Writing the Critical Essay

Recycling

An OPPOSING VIEWPOINTS® Guide

Lauri S. Friedman, *Book Editor*

OPPOSING
VIEWPOINTS®
SERIES

GREENHAVEN PRESS
A part of Gale, Cengage Learning

GALE
CENGAGE Learning™

Detroit • New York • San Francisco • New Haven, Conn • Waterville, Maine • London

GALE
CENGAGE Learning

Christine Nasso, *Publisher*
Elizabeth Des Chenes, *Managing Editor*

© 2010 Greenhaven Press, a part of Gale, Cengage Learning

Gale and Greenhaven Press are registered trademarks used herein under license.

For more information, contact:
Greenhaven Press
27500 Drake Rd.
Farmington Hills, MI 48331-3535
Or you can visit our Internet site at gale.cengage.com

For product information and technology assistance, contact us at

Gale Customer Support, 1-800-877-4253
For permission to use material from this text or product, submit all requests online at www.cengage.com/permissions

Further permissions questions can be e-mailed to permissionrequest@cengage.com

Articles in Greenhaven Press anthologies are often edited for length to meet page requirements. In addition, original titles of these works are changed to clearly present the main thesis and to explicitly indicate the author's opinion. Every effort is made to ensure that Greenhaven Press accurately reflects the original intent of the authors. Every effort has been made to trace the owners of copyrighted material.

Cover image © Jason Gallier/Alamy

LIBRARY OF CONGRESS CATALOGING-IN-PUBLICATION DATA

Recycling / Lauri S. Friedman, book editor.
    p. cm. -- (Writing the critical essay, an opposing viewpoints guide)
Includes bibliographical references and index.
ISBN 978-0-7377-4803-1 (hardcover)
1. Recycling (Waste, etc.) 2. Recycling (Waste, etc.)--Economic aspects. 3. Waste products. I. Friedman, Lauri S.
TD794.5.R4195 2010
363.72'82--dc22
                                                                    2010000263

Printed in the United States of America
1 2 3 4 5 6 7 14 13 12 11 10

CONTENTS

Foreword 5

Introduction 7

    Is Recycling a Significant or Superficial
Environmental Gesture?

Section One: Opposing Viewpoints on Recycling

Viewpoint One: Recycling Is Environmentally Friendly   12
Tom Zeller Jr.

Viewpoint Two: Recycling Is Not Always
Environmentally Friendly   18
Rachel Cernansky

Viewpoint Three: Recycling Saves Energy   25
Greg Wittbecker

Viewpoint Four: Recycling Wastes Energy   32
James Thayer

Viewpoint Five: Recycling Should Be Mandatory   40
Marc Gunther

Viewpoint Six: Recycling Should Not Be Mandatory   48
Michael D. Shaw

Section Two: Model Essays and Writing Exercises

Preface A: The Five-Paragraph Essay   55

Preface B: The Descriptive Essay   57

Essay One: Recycling Is Ineffective   60
    Exercise 1A: Create an Outline from an
            Existing Essay   63
    Exercise 1B: Create an Outline for Your
            Own Essay   64

Essay Two: The Wisdom of Toilet-to-Tap 67

 Exercise 2A: Create an Outline from an
   Existing Essay 70

 Exercise 2B: Examining Introductions
   and Conclusions 70

 Exercise 2C: Using Quotations to Enliven
   Your Essay 72

Essay Three: Students Seek Recycling on Campus 73

 Exercise 3A: Conducting an Interview 78

 Exercise 3B: Report on an Event 80

Final Writing Challenge: Write Your Own
Descriptive Five-Paragraph Essay 82

Section Three: Supporting Research Material

Appendix A: Facts About Recycling 86

Appendix B: Finding and Using Sources of
Information 90

Appendix C: Using MLA Style to Create a Works
Cited List 94

Appendix D: Sample Essay Topics 97

Organizations to Contact 98

Bibliography 103

Index 107

Picture Credits 110

About the Editor 111

Examining the state of writing and how it is taught in the United States was the official purpose of the National Commission on Writing in America's Schools and Colleges. The commission, made up of teachers, school administrators, business leaders, and college and university presidents, released its first report in 2003. "Despite the best efforts of many educators," commissioners argued, "writing has not received the full attention it deserves." Among the findings of the commission was that most fourth-grade students spent less than three hours a week writing, that three-quarters of high school seniors never receive a writing assignment in their history or social studies classes, and that more than 50 percent of first-year students in college have problems writing error-free papers. The commission called for a "cultural sea change" that would increase the emphasis on writing for both elementary and secondary schools. These conclusions have made some educators realize that writing must be emphasized in the curriculum. As colleges are demanding an ever-higher level of writing proficiency from incoming students, schools must respond by making students more competent writers. In response to these concerns, the SAT, an influential standardized test used for college admissions, required an essay for the first time in 2005.

Books in the Writing the Critical Essay: An Opposing Viewpoints Guide series use the patented Opposing Viewpoints format to help students learn to organize ideas and arguments and to write essays using common critical writing techniques. Each book in the series focuses on a particular type of essay writing—including expository, persuasive, descriptive, and narrative—that students learn while being taught both the five-paragraph essay as well as longer pieces of writing that have an opinionated focus. These guides include everything necessary to help students research, outline, draft, edit, and ultimately write successful essays across the curriculum, including essays for the SAT.

Using Opposing Viewpoints

This series is inspired by and builds upon Greenhaven Press's acclaimed Opposing Viewpoints series. As in the parent series, each book in the Writing the Critical Essay series focuses on a timely and controversial social issue that provides lots of opportunities for creating thought-provoking essays. The first section of each volume begins with a brief introductory essay that provides context for the opposing viewpoints that follow. These articles are chosen for their accessibility and clearly stated views. The thesis of each article is made explicit in the article's title and is accentuated by its pairing with an opposing or alternative view. These essays are both models of persuasive writing techniques and valuable research material that students can mine to write their own informed essays. Guided reading and discussion questions help lead students to key ideas and writing techniques presented in the selections.

The second section of each book begins with a preface discussing the format of the essays and examining characteristics of the featured essay type. Model five-paragraph and longer essays then demonstrate that essay type. The essays are annotated so that key writing elements and techniques are pointed out to the student. Sequential, step-by-step exercises help students construct and refine thesis statements; organize material into outlines; analyze and try out writing techniques; write transitions, introductions, and conclusions; and incorporate quotations and other researched material. Ultimately, students construct their own compositions using the designated essay type.

The third section of each volume provides additional research material and writing prompts to help the student. Additional facts about the topic of the book serve as a convenient source of supporting material for essays. Other features help students go beyond the book for their research. Like other Greenhaven Press books, each book in the Writing the Critical Essay series includes bibliographic listings of relevant periodical articles, books, Web sites, and organizations to contact.

Writing the Critical Essay: An Opposing Viewpoints Guide will help students master essay techniques that can be used in any discipline.

Is Recycling a Significant or Superficial Environmental Gesture?

In 2008 two nationwide polls revealed something very curious about the way Americans view recycling. One poll, jointly conducted by ABC News, Planet Green, and Stanford University, asked Americans what they thought was the biggest environmental problem the world faces. Lack of recycling or too much waste ranked very low on the list—just 4 percent of Americans thought that not enough recycling and/or too much waste qualified as a serious environmental problem. Yet when a Gallup poll that same year asked Americans what changes they had personally made in their shopping and living habits to help protect the environment, recycling *topped* the list. This time, 39 percent of respondents said that in the past year they had started to recycle or recycled more than they used to. The second closest answer was carpooling, which 17 percent of Americans said they did.

These results suggest a contradiction in American thinking: On the one hand, the majority of people participate in recycling efforts; yet on the other, very few think that recycling is one of the more important environmental steps that needs to be taken. In other words, even though they do not believe that too much waste or not enough recycling is a huge problem, people recycle anyway. This kind of behavior has led some to speculate that Americans recycle because it is a feel-good, easy activity that makes them feel like they are doing something good for the planet, even when they do not view the action as all that important. Whether recycling is a significant or superficial environmental gesture is hotly debated by commentators, analysts, policy makers, environmentalists, and other key people in the field.

People like Greg Wittbecker never question the benefit of recycling. Wittbecker is the director of the Corporate Recycling Strategy at Alcoa, Inc., the world's leading producer of aluminum products. According to Wittbecker and his organization, recycling materials such as aluminum saves enormous quantities of energy and prevents raw materials from needing to be harvested. For example, recycling one ton of aluminum uses just 5 percent of the energy it takes to make new aluminum from scratch. That is a savings of fourteen thousand kilowatt hours of electricity per ton of recycled aluminum—the equivalent of the amount of power it takes to run an American home for fifteen months. As Americans face higher energy prices, energy shortfalls, and environmental harm (such as climate change and air pollution) from their energy use, any tool that helps them use less energy should be embraced, argues Wittbecker. "Whether it's aluminum beverage cans, telephone books and newspapers, or plastic shopping bags, recycling has a common and vital benefit: energy conservation. And it's one that can resonate with the average American."[1]

On the other hand, recycling has been criticized by opponents who say it consumes more resources than it preserves. For example, recycling expends energy by requiring more trucks to drive around picking up trash and hauling it to a recycling center. Processing the recycled materials and creating new material out of them uses further energy. As engineer and *Machine Design* editor Leland E. Teschler says:

> Sending around city trucks to pick up glass, paper, and plastic actually consumes more energy than it saves. And it may even pollute the air more than just pitching this stuff in the trash. A little thought shows why. It takes as many trucks to collect perhaps four to eight pounds of recyclables that a typical household generates as it does to pickup the 40 pounds of refuse created by the same residence.[2]

Some say this energy use is inexcusable considering that most of the products that get recycled—such as glass, plastic, and paper—are not in any danger of being depleted. Says Jay Lehr, science director of the Heartland Institute, "We are not running out of, nor will we ever run out of, any of the resources we recycle."[3] Indeed, glass—which is composed primarily of sand—is abundant on Earth; much of the plastic that gets recycled is made from synthetic products; and much of the paper that gets recycled is made from trees in forests that have been planted specifically for the purpose of harvesting paper.

Lehr and others suggest that recycling is popular because Americans get a "warm and fuzzy feeling when we recycle"[4] but fail to consider that their efforts are largely a waste of time, money, effort, and energy. Indeed, in places with curbside recycling programs and conveniently located bins, the act takes mere seconds. Christian Lander, author of the popular book and blog *Stuff White People Like*, has joked about this easy, feel-good quality of recycling: "Recycling is fantastic!" he writes. "You can still buy all the stuff you like (bottled water, beer, wine, organic iced tea, and cans of all varieties) and then when you're done you just put it in a DIFFERENT bin than where you would throw your other garbage. And boom! Environment saved! Everyone feels great, it's so easy!"[5]

Yet supporters of recycling think that to use an item two or three times or even infinitely (as is the case with recycled aluminum), rather than adopt a use-it-once-and-throw-it-away mentality, simply makes common sense. While recycling some items makes more sense than recycling others, doing so can save energy, time, money, and create jobs and industries that revolve around recycled products. "Consider the true cost of a product over its entire life—from harvesting the raw materials to creating, consuming, and disposing of it—and the scale tips dramatically in recycling's favor,"[6] says reporter Tom Zeller Jr.

Whether recycling is truly a significant environmental act or is a merely superficial feel-good gesture is just one of the many issues explored in *Writing the Critical Essay: Recycling*. Readers will also consider arguments about whether recycling is cost-effective, whether it saves or wastes energy, and what role the government should play in guiding Americans' recycling habits. These issues are explored in passionately argued viewpoints and model essays. Thought-provoking writing exercises and step-by-step instructions help readers write their own five-paragraph descriptive essays on this compelling and multifaceted subject.

Notes

1. Greg Wittbecker, "Recycle to Save Energy—the Sooner the Better," *Environmental Leader*, May 13, 2008.
2. Leland E. Teschler, "Save Energy: Don't Recycle," *Machine Design*, July 13, 2006.
3. Quoted in James Thayer, "Recycle This! Separating Tin Cans and Pizza Boxes and Exposing the Facts About the High Church of Recycling," *Weekly Standard*, January 26, 2006.
4. Quoted in Thayer, "Recycle This!"
5. Christian Lander, *Stuff White People Like*. New York: Random House, 2008, p. 79.
6. Tom Zeller Jr., "Recycling: The Big Picture," *National Geographic*, January 2008, p. 82.

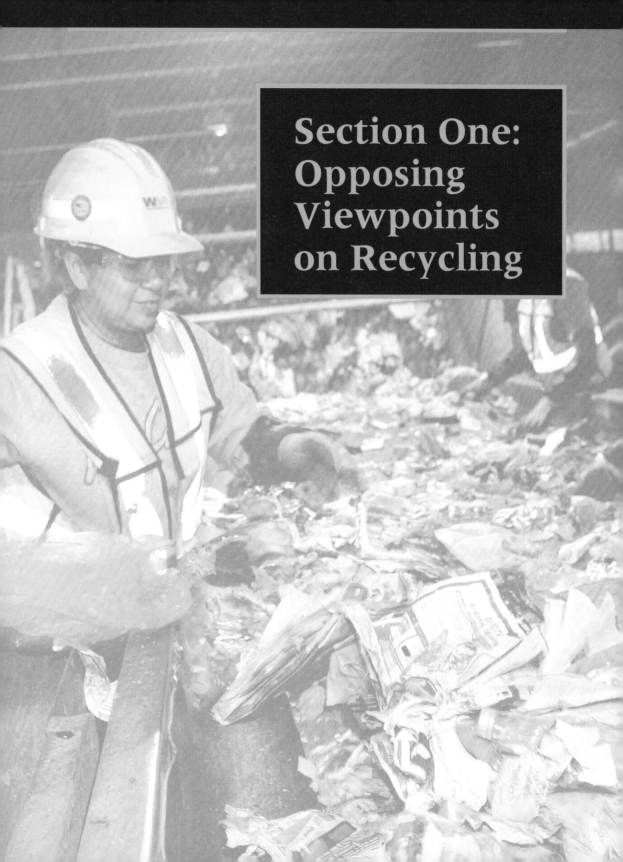

Section One:
Opposing
Viewpoints
on Recycling

Recycling Is Environmentally Friendly

Tom Zeller Jr.

In the following essay Tom Zeller Jr. explains that recycling is environmentally friendly. Zeller thinks the benefits of recycling are clear when one considers the total and true cost of a product—that is, the money, energy, and pollution required to make and dispose of it. When one takes into account the raw materials that go into creating a product, the energy used and pollution emitted in this process, and the costs of consuming and disposing of it, Zeller says recycling is a very cost-effective and environmentally friendly way to deal with the growing amount of waste on the planet. He says the United States has successfully recycled certain kinds of products but suggests it needs to efficiently recycle more kinds of products.

Zeller is a writer whose articles have appeared in the *New York Times* and *National Geographic*, where this essay was originally printed.

Consider the following questions:

1. What percent of all lead-acid batteries are recycled, according to Zeller?
2. What, according to the author, is the concept of "extended producer responsibility"?
3. What does the author say is the recycling rate in Denmark and Sweden?

Tom Zeller Jr., "Recycling: The Big Picture," *National Geographic*, vol. 213, January 2008, pp. 82-87. Copyright © 2008 National Geographic Society. Reproduced by permission.

D oes It make sense to recycle?
The short answer is: Yes.

A Product's True Cost

True, some critics wonder whether mandatory programs are a net benefit, since they can require more trucks consuming energy and belching carbon dioxide into the atmosphere.

"You don't want a large truck carrying around just a few bottles," concedes Matthew Hale, director of EPA's [Environmental Protection Agency's] Office of Solid Waste. But, he notes, most cities are getting better at reducing the environmental costs of recycling. (They're also working to reduce the economic costs. Many recycling programs still cost more to run than they bring in when they sell the recyclable materials back to manufacturers.)

Consider the true cost of a product over its entire life— from harvesting the raw materials to creating, consuming, and disposing of it—and the scale tips dramatically in recycling's favor. Every shrink-wrapped toy or tool or medical device we buy bears the stamp of its energy-intensive history: mountains of ore that have been mined (bauxite, say, for aluminum cans), coal plants and oil refineries, railcars, assembly lines. A product's true cost includes greenhouse gases emitted in its creation as well as use, and pollutants that cause acid rain, smog, and fouled waterways.

Recycling Conserves Resources

Recycling—substituting scrap for virgin materials—not only conserves natural resources and reduces the amount of waste that must be burned or buried, it also reduces pollution and the demand for energy. "You get tremendous Btu [energy] savings," Hale says.

In an international study published last year [2007] by the Waste & Resources Action Programme, a British group, researchers compared more than 180 municipal waste management systems. Recycling proved better for the environment than burying or burning waste in 83 percent of the cases.

It makes sense to reuse products, of course, and to reduce consumption altogether, as well as to improve initial product design. But given the rising mounds of waste worldwide, it also makes sense to recycle.

What Makes Most Sense to Recycle?

Whether or not a particular material is recycled depends on a number of factors, but the most fundamental question is this: Is there a market for it? Markets for some materials, like car batteries, are highly developed and efficient—not least because strict regulations govern their disposal—and a mature recycling infrastructure has grown up as a result. About 90 percent of all lead-acid batteries are recycled, according to the EPA. Steel recycling, too, has been around for decades, while formalized recycling of yard trimmings has not. Despite the explosive growth of plastics—particularly for use in beverage containers—that industry has been slow to develop a recycling infrastructure, with most plastic still going to incinerators or landfills.

Higher hygiene standards, smaller households, intense brand marketing, and the rise of ready-made meals have all contributed to an increase in packaging waste, but international trade may be the biggest factor. Even simple items like bottles of water now routinely crisscross the globe, meaning that thirst for a few swallows of "product" can generate not just plastic bottles, but also a large amount of other packaging debris—from wrapping film to bin liners to shipping crates.

The Benefits of Recycling

Britain's recycling efforts reduce its carbon-dioxide emissions by 10–15 million tons per year [which is] equivalent to taking 3.5 million cars off the roads.... Recycling has many other benefits, too. It conserves natural resources. It also reduces the amount of waste that is buried or burnt, hardly ideal ways to get rid of the stuff.

Economist, "The Truth About Recycling," vol. 383, no. 8532, June 7, 2007.

From tin cans to milk cartons, there are a number of materials to recycle and market in today's race to be environmentally friendly.

The United States Should Look to Europe

So far, Europe has led the world in recycling packaging materials—principally through the Packaging and Packaging Waste Directive of 1994. The EU [European Union] directive calls for manufacturers, retailers, and others in the product chain to share the recycling burden.

With the exception of hazardous wastes, the United States has been slower to embrace the concept of "extended producer responsibility," as the idea is known, according to Bill Sheehan, director of the Product Policy Institute, a nonprofit research organization in Athens, Georgia. Some municipalities, however, are starting to

America Recycles More Each Year

The amount of solid waste in the United States has nearly tripled in the past half-century, to 251 million tons. During the same period, the amount of waste recycled—including composting—increased more than fifteen fold, to 82 million tons.

Management of Municipal Solid Waste, 1960–2006

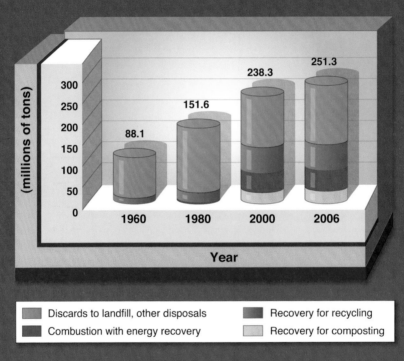

Taken from: "Municipal Solid Waste Generation, Recycling, and Disposal in the United States: Facts and Figures for 2006," Environmental Protection Agency.

demand that businesses help cover the costs of recycling. "Otherwise," Sheehan says, we are "just stimulating the production of more stuff."

According to European Union officials, countries such as Denmark and Sweden, which recycle nearly all their own consumption of a material, can appear to have a recycling rate above 100 percent when they also import waste to be recycled from other countries.

Analyze the essay:

1. Zeller talks about the amount of materials that go into the creation and disposal of plastic water bottles, suggesting that all this material is hardly worth using for just a few "swallows of product." Think of the most and least environmentally friendly products you consume on a daily or weekly basis. How much packaging do they come in? Do you recycle or reuse any part of it?

2. The author suggests three ways that waste can be reduced: by reusing products, improving their design, and/or recycling. Of these three options, which do you think makes most financial and environmental sense? Why?

Recycling Is Not Always Environmentally Friendly

Rachel Cernansky

Recycling is not always good for the environment, argues Rachel Cernansky in the following essay. She explains that plastic is a very complex material that cannot always be easily recycled. Many plastics are made of combinations of materials—while some of these can be safely recycled, others cannot and it is difficult to know when a plastic has unrecyclable materials in it. Sorting plastics for recycling has become more challenging now that so many different materials go into plastic production, she says. When plastic contains unrecyclable materials, it actually contaminates whole batches of recycled plastic. For all these reasons, Cernansky says that sometimes throwing away certain types of plastics instead of recycling them is more environmentally friendly and cost-efficient.

Cernansky is a writer and environmentalist. She was assistant editor of *Satya*, a New York–based magazine focused on the environment, animal rights, and social justice.

Consider the following questions:

1. When does recycling a yogurt container do more harm than throwing it away, according to the author?
2. What does Cernansky say is the problem with recycling some #1 and #2 plastics?
3. What effect does Cernansky say environmentally friendly bioplastics have had on recycling efforts?

Rachel Cernansky, "When Recycling Is Bad for the Environment," *Discover Magazine*, July 6, 2009. Copyright © 2009 The Walt Disney Company. Reproduced by permission.

You just polished off some yogurt and, because of that chasing-arrows symbol on the bottom of the container, you assume it should go in the recycle bin. Right? Not necessarily.

When Recycling Does More Harm than Good

Glass, metal, and paper are pretty straightforward, but when it comes to plastic, things get tricky. The truth is that what you can recycle depends on where you live and what materials your city's facilities can handle. There are many different types of plastic, and they cannot all be recycled together. So unless you're diligent about sorting all your plastics, then "recycling" that yogurt container may be doing more harm than simply throwing it away.

Distinguishing between the various types of plastic makes recycling complicated.

Recycling is generally far better than sending waste to landfills and relying on new raw materials to drive the consumer economy. It takes two-thirds less energy to make products from recycled plastic than from virgin plastic. By the last official measure in 2005, Americans recycle an estimated 32 percent of their total waste, which averages nearly a ton per person per year, around a third of which is plastic. Our recycling efforts save the greenhouse gas equivalent of removing 39.6 million cars from the road.

But not all plastic can be recycled, and only about 6.8 percent of the total plastic used in the U.S. actually goes that route—although the rate is higher with bottles: 37 percent for soft drink and 28 percent for milk and water bottles.

> ## It Takes Energy and Resources to Recycle
>
> Recycling requires twice as many trucks, twice as much gas consumption, and thus twice as much atmospheric pollution.
>
> Lucas McMillan, "Recycling's Myth: The 'Three R's' Are Doing More Harm than Good," *Times-Delphic* [Drake University], November 19, 2007.

Plastic Is Too Complex to Be Simply Recycled

The chief problem lies in plastic's complexity: There are as many types of plastic as there are uses. And since each type can only be recycled with its own kind, plastics need to be carefully sorted before they can be processed. The presence of enough foreign materials—from food to dissimilar kinds of plastic—can ruin an entire batch of would-be recyclables.

Plastics are chemically categorized by numbers, which are displayed inside the chasing-arrow icon on many plastic containers. The two most common types are plastic #1 (polyethylene terephthalate, or PETE), which is used mainly in soda and water bottles, and #2 (high-density polyethylene, or HDPE), used in things like detergent bottles and milk jugs. Unfortunately, while plastics marked #1 or #2 are generally considered to be recyclable, not all containers with those numbers actually are.

Recycling Not High on Americans' List of Environmental Priorities

A 2008 survey of Americans revealed that very few consider not enough recycling to be a pressing environmental problem.

"What in your opinion is the single biggest environmental problem the world faces at this time?"

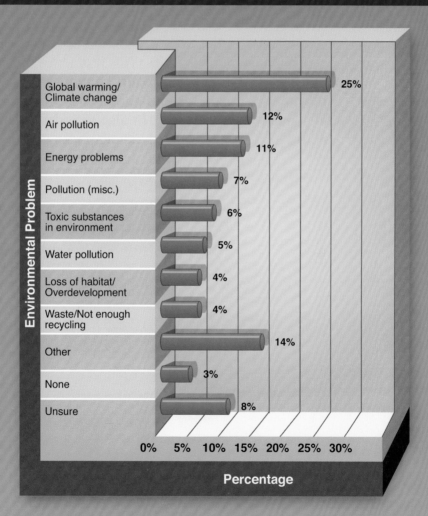

Note: numbers do not total 100 due to rounding.

Taken from: ABC News/Planet Green/Stanford University poll, July 23–28, 2008.

The reason for this is that many plastics contain additives blended into the original resin, and the different additives create discrepancies even within each category. Every container in the grocery store is made with a unique blend of chemicals—plasticizers, molding agents, dyes—that combine to give a plastic its shape, color, strength, and flexibility (or lack thereof). As a result, they melt at varying temperatures and respond differently to new additives, and so they cannot all be melted down and recycled together to make a new product.

As a result, most plastic, aside from the ubiquitous clear plastic bottle, cannot, generally speaking, be recycled by most municipalities. This problem applies to the #1s and #2s, as well as yogurt containers or hummus tubs, and Chinese-takeout containers, which are usually made from #5 plastic. (It also includes plastic bags and the frustratingly hard plastic packaging that your

Sorting is crucial in the recycling process. Sorting materials must often be done by hand as shown at the Sacramento Recycling and Transfer Station, in Sacramento, California.

headphones came in, which don't even earn a recycling number.) But many people don't know that, so they toss all of them in the blue bin, thereby reducing efficiency at the sorting plant, which is where your plastic goes when it's collected on recycling day.

Contamination in the Recycle Bin

Sorting is a crucial part of the recycling process. Plastic sorting can be done manually, but it's tedious and labor-intensive. Automatic sorting is far more efficient, but the technology is not foolproof: There are so many types of plastics that sorting equipment can't look for all possible additives in the materials passing through. (Ironically, the increasing use of bio-plastics—which are made from renewable materials like cornstarch and are meant to be more earth-friendly than conventional oil-based plastic—has made the job of automatic sorting machines even harder.)

Any contamination in the recycle bin compromises the strength and durability of the recycled plastic that is produced, which in turn compromises its future use as a material for manufacturers. A recycled container needs to be strong enough to hold the weight of the contents inside, and many container shapes already contain weak spots where the plastic has a reduced thickness—near a bottle's handle, for example.

While all these complications make it difficult to produce containers with a high percentage of recycled plastic, some companies are still taking on the challenge. Seventh Generation, a company that makes eco-friendly household products, is increasing the recycled content of all its packaging, with a goal of 75 percent for all products by the end of [2009].

Some Plastics Should Just Be Thrown Out

But Seventh Generation is an exception to a widespread industry trend. It is virtually impossible to calculate the industry average for how much recycled plastic goes into packaging, according to Tom Outerbridge, director of municipal recycling for Sims Metal Management, a metals and electronics recycling company. Without a built-in environmental ethic like the one Seventh Generation has, individual companies are inconsistent in their use of recycled content, and can use anywhere from zero to 100 percent recycled plastic in their products. But when the quality of the recycled plastic goes down, so does that percentage.

So if you're wondering if you should continue to recycle your plastics, here's an answer: Yes. But before you do, educate yourself on which plastics your city collects, and bring other types to outlets where they can be properly sorted. If you're unsure about a plastic—old CD jewel boxes, perhaps, or Saran Wrap—then putting it in the bin and hoping it will be recycled anyway does nothing for the environment. It's going to be thrown into the garbage after an elaborate and costly sorting process, so you might as well just toss it out yourself.

Analyze the essay:

1. Cernansky uses facts and examples to make her point that recycling is not always environmentally friendly. She does not, however, use any quotations to support her ideas. If you were to rewrite this essay and insert quotations, what authorities might you quote from? Where would you place these quotations to bolster the points Cernansky makes?

2. In the previous essay Tom Zeller Jr. suggests Americans should be like the Danes and the Swedes, who recycle 100 percent of their waste. How do you think Cernansky would respond to this suggestion?

Recycling Saves Energy

Greg Wittbecker

In the following essay Greg Wittbecker argues that recycling can save large quantities of energy. He says that recycling aluminum and making new products from it uses just a tiny fraction of the energy required to make aluminum from raw materials. For example, Wittbecker says the energy saved by recycling just one ton of aluminum could power the average American household for fifteen months. Wittbecker wants people to realize that recycling can save them not just energy but money. He says America is fully capable of recycling more of its aluminum and other materials and should do so in order to save energy, money, and the environment.

Wittbecker is the director of the Corporate Recycling Strategy at Alcoa, Inc., the world's leading producer of aluminum products.

Consider the following questions:

1. How much energy does Wittbecker say could be saved if the United States recycled 75 percent of its aluminum cans?
2. Recycling one ton of aluminum requires what percent of the energy needed to make new aluminum, according to Wittbecker?
3. What percent of its aluminum does Wittbecker say America currently recycles? How does this compare with Brazil, Japan, and Germany?

Greg Wittbecker, "Recycling to Save Energy—the Sooner the Better," *Environmental Leader*, May 13, 2008. Copyright © 2006-2009 Environmental Leader LLC. All rights reserved. Reproduced by permission.

Recycling rates in the U.S. are low and getting lower. The U.S., by far the world's biggest consumer of aluminum cans, lags behind other industrialized nations in the percentage of these cans that we recycle. This is despite the fact that the number of cans sold is fairly constant.

Saving Tons of Energy

If we could recover and recycle 75% of the aluminum cans being currently tossed into landfills—600,000 metric tons of aluminum—we could save 1286 megawatts of generated electricity. That's the amount produced by two coal fired power plants, and consumed by two aluminum plants. Replacing this production with recycling would keep 11.8 million metric tons of carbon dioxide from being generated and released into the atmosphere.

All by just recycling, instead of throwing away, one of the most successful packaging solutions ever devised—the aluminum beverage can.

Recycling aluminum has always been a sustainable practice because it saves landfill space. Even more important in today's environment, recycling also saves energy. In fact, because of the way aluminum is made and the ease with which you can recycle it, recycling saves a lot of energy . . . which makes recycling an important component of climate change action and a sound economic practice as well.

Aluminum Can Be Infinitely Recycled

Since the modern process for producing aluminum was developed by Alcoa founder Charles Martin Hall in 1886, over 70% of all the virgin aluminum ever made remains in use. That's because aluminum can be infinitely recycled—a piece of aluminum scrap can often be turned

Recycling Offers Enormous Savings

When one ton of steel is recycled, 2,500 pounds of iron ore, 1,400 pounds of coal, and 120 pounds of limestone are conserved. Recycling a ton of paper saves 7,000 gallons of water.

City of Fort Collins, Colorado, "Why Recycling Matters." www.fcgov.com.

back into the same product, or a very similar product, to that from which it originated, with virtually no material loss in the process. Aluminum truly can be a model for sustainability in heavy industry.

Recycling aluminum saves energy that can be used to power households.

Saving Energy Means Saving Money

Scrap usage is also driven by economics. Recycling aluminum scrap saves enormous quantities of energy, otherwise required to make virgin aluminum. Recycling a ton of aluminum uses just 5% of the energy required to make virgin metal. Every ton of recycled aluminum that Alcoa uses saves about 14,000 kilowatt hours of electricity. The U.S. Energy Information Administration (EIA) estimates that the average American household consumes 920 kilowatts of electricity per month. Consequently, using 1 ton of recycled aluminum as opposed to 1 ton of virgin aluminum would power an American household for over 15 months.

Recycled Content Saves Energy

Products made with recycled material often require far less energy than making the same products with virgin content. Aluminum cans, for example, require about 8 million BTUs if made with recycled material versus 229 million BTUs using virgin materials.

Energy Usage of Products Made with Virgin Versus Recycled Content

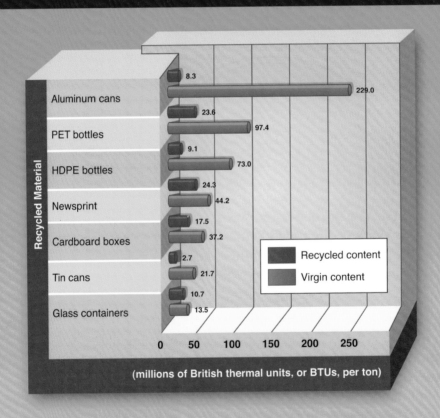

Taken from: Sound Resource Management.

This comparison is one that the average American can relate to. The timing also couldn't be better for pointing it out. There isn't anyone in this country who has not felt the effect of the massive increase in energy costs in the past year. Industries like Alcoa feel it too. It stands to reason that IF we can reduce energy consumption by recycling more, we can remove some of the demand pull that is causing energy prices to rise. And with much of the energy in the U.S. still coming from fossil fuel generation, we can move toward a reduced national carbon footprint as well.

America Lags Behind the Rest of the World

Despite the compelling energy savings that accrue from recycling aluminum, we Americans are not realizing our recycling potential. Currently, just over 50% of the aluminum beverage cans consumed in this country are being recycled. This is well below world standards:

- Brazil 94.4%
- Japan 90.9%
- Germany 89%
- Global Average 63%
- Western Europe 57.7%

The reasons for the malaise in our recycling rates are complex: bad behavior (we would rather dispose than recycle or reuse); a lack of convenient recycling options at home, office or other public venues; local governments lacking funding to provide recycling infrastructure; and, at least until recently, some apathy about the green movement.

A Challenge to Do Better

Alcoa began the can recycling industry in the 1970s shortly after the aluminum can was introduced, and has been able to recycle 30 billion cans, equaling nearly half a million tons of aluminum, since then. That sounds like a lot—and it is—but it's just 30% of the total number of new cans shipped by the industry each year.

Certainly, for everyone involved, there's plenty of room for improvement. In a recent call to action, I issued a challenge for Alcoa, "to raise recycling rates from the current 52% to 75% by 2015."

That's a big challenge . . . equating to capturing another 400,000 tons/year of aluminum cans. However, it's a goal that we can and must achieve if we want more sustainability in our industry. It's also a vital contribution that the aluminum industry can make towards comprehensive energy conservation.

America lags behind the rest of the world when it comes to recycling and reusing aluminum. In Russia aluminum is recycled to create ingots, casted aluminum bars or blocks created for industry uses.

We Must Use Recycling to Conserve Energy

While Alcoa is an aluminum company, we recognize that there are other valuable materials that can be recycled, affording even more substantial energy savings. . . .

Clearly, besides aluminum . . . there are a lot of kilowatts and barrels of oil waiting to be saved through a

comprehensive approach to recycling. Whether it's aluminum beverage cans, telephone books and newspapers, or plastic shopping bags, recycling has a common and vital benefit: energy conservation. And it's one that can resonate with the average American.

Analyze the essay:

1. The author of this essay is an executive at Alcoa, Inc., the world's leading producer of aluminum products. How does knowing his professional background influence your opinion of his argument? Explain your reasoning.

2. Wittbecker discusses the reasons why Americans do not recycle more. What are these reasons? What is your opinion of them? Suggest at least one way Americans could be convinced to recycle more based on what Wittbecker has described.

Recycling Wastes Energy

James Thayer

Recycling does not save energy or resources, argues James Thayer in the following essay. He explains that Americans have adopted recycling because it makes them feel like they are doing something good for the planet—but in reality, says Thayer, recycling is a waste of money and energy. Recycling requires more trucks to be used to haul garbage to multiple sites, which wastes gas. Then, processing the recycled materials and delivering them to manufacturing plants consumes further amounts of energy. Thayer says this waste is all for nothing, since most of the products that get recycled are not in danger of being depleted. Thayer says landfills have plenty of room for garbage, and that is where recyclables should be sent. He concludes that recycling consumes energy and offers Americans little or nothing in return.

Thayer is a writer whose articles have appeared in the *Weekly Standard*, a conservative news magazine in which this essay was originally printed.

Consider the following questions:

1. According to Thayer, how much does it cost per ton to recycle in New York City? How much does it cost to send this waste to a landfill?
2. How many more garbage trucks does Thayer say Los Angeles needs to operate due to its recycling program?
3. What percent of America's paper comes from renewable forests, according to Thayer?

Seattle's proudly progressive leaders were alarmed when, almost two decades after voluntary recycling programs were initiated in the city—recycling rates had stalled at about 40 percent of the total amount of waste. Too many bottles and too much paper were still finding their way to the eastern Oregon landfill that receives Seattle's garbage.

So after a year-long $450,000 television, radio and newspaper education campaign, [a] mandatory recycling law went into effect [in 2006]. The goal is to raise the percentage of recyclables to sixty percent of total waste. Seattle is not alone, of course; many other cities, from Philadelphia to Honolulu, also have mandatory recycling programs. But these laws are based on myth and followed as faith.

Recycling causes companies to spend money and time processing recycled goods.

Recycling Is Too Expensive

Echoing widespread Seattle sentiment (85 percent of the city's citizens approve of curbside recycling), the *Seattle Times* editorial board has concluded that "Recycling is a good thing." After all, using a bottle twice must be better than using it once, saving resources and sparing the landfill.

The truth, though, is that recycling is an expense, not a savings, for a city. "Every community recycling pro-

Recycling Rates Around the World

The United States does not recycle as much as other industrialized nations. Proponents of recycling say it should do more.

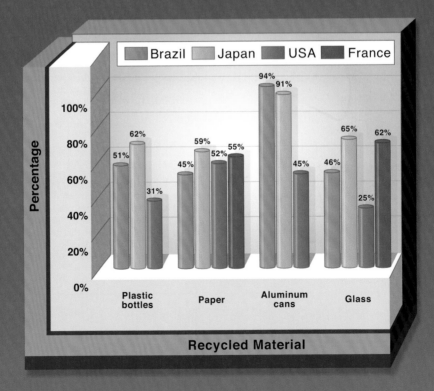

gram in America today costs more than the revenue it generates," says Dr. Jay Lehr of the Heartland Institute.

A telling indicator is that cities often try to dump recycling programs when budgets are tight. As Angela Logomasini, director of risk and environmental policy at the Competitive Enterprise Institute, points out in the *Wall Street Journal*, every New York City mayor has attempted to stop the city's recycling program since it was begun in 1989. Mayor David Dinkins tried, but changed his mind when met with noisy criticism. Rudy Giuliani tried, but was sued by the Natural Resources Defense Council, which won the case. Mayor [Michael] Bloomberg has proposed temporarily ending the recycling program because, as Logomasini notes, it costs $240 per ton to recycle and only $130 per ton to send the material to a landfill. The numbers for other areas are roughly comparable. The net per-ton cost of recycling exceeds $180 in Rhode Island, while conventional garbage collection and disposal costs $120 to $160 per ton.

> ## Recycling Is Bad for the Environment
>
> Sending around city trucks to pick up glass, paper, and plastic actually consumes more energy than it saves. And it may even pollute the air more than just pitching this stuff in the trash. A little thought shows why. It takes as many trucks to collect perhaps four to eight pounds of recyclables that a typical household generates as it does to pickup the 40 pounds of refuse created by the same residence.
>
> Leland E. Teschler, "Save Energy: Don't Recycle," *Machine Design*, July 13, 2006.

More Trucks, More Gas, More Waste

The funds go for trucks and collectors and inspectors and bureaucrats. Clemson professor Daniel K. Benjamin points out that Los Angeles has 800 trucks working the neighborhoods, instead of 400, due to recycling. Radley Balko at aBetterEarth.Org, a project of the Institute for Humane Studies at George Mason University, writes, "That means extra wear and tear on city streets, double the exhaust emissions into the atmosphere, double the man hours required for someone to drive and man those trucks, and double the costs of maintenance and upkeep of the trucks."

Jerry Taylor of the Cato Institute says costs include "the energy necessary to deliver the recyclables to the collection centers, process the post-consumer material into usable commodities for manufacturers, and deliver the processed post-consumer material to manufacturing plants." Franklin Associates, which provides consulting services for solid waste management, estimates that curbside recycling is 55 percent more expensive, pound for pound, than conventional garbage disposal. . . .

We Are Not Running Out of Landfill Space

If we weren't recycling, wouldn't the landfills soon overflow? Al Gore certainly thinks so, as he claimed we are "running out of ways to dispose of our waste in a manner that keeps it out of either sight or mind." Nonsense. Clemson Professor Daniel K. Benjamin notes that rather than running out of space, overall capacity is growing. "In fact," he says, "the United States today has more landfill capacity than ever before." He adds that the total land area required to contain every scrap of this country's garbage for the next 100 years would be only 10 miles square. The Nevada Policy Research Institute's numbers are even more dramatic: an area 44 miles square and 120 feet deep would handle all of America's garbage for the next millennium.

America's image of landfills was fixed decades ago, and is that of Staten Island's Fresh Kills, a vast swampy expanse of detritus, with huge Caterpillar tractors trundling over it, and clouds of seagulls obscuring everything above ground. Fresh Kills received New York's garbage for 53 years before it was closed in 2001. Modern landfills have nothing in common with the place. Benjamin says that new landfills are located far from groundwater supplies, and are built on thick clay beds that are covered with plastic liners, on top of which goes another layer of sand or gravel. Pipes remove leachate, which is then treated at wastewater plants. Escaping gas is

burned or sold. A park or golf course or industrial development eventually goes over the landfill.

Fresh Kills also looked dangerous, a veritable soup of deadly poisons and nasty chemicals, seeping and dissolving and dispersing. But that's not the case with new landfills. Daniel Benjamin writes, "According to the EPA's [Environmental Protection Agency's] own estimates, modern landfills can be expected to cause 5.7 cancer-related deaths over the next 300 years—just one death every 50 years. To put this in perspective, cancer kills over 560,000 people every year in the United States."

More garbage and recycling trucks are used today due to laws that require cities to separate garbage, recyclables, and compost into different bins. The increased use of trucks wastes gas and causes more air pollution.

Resources Are Not Saved by Recycling

But what about saving precious resources by recycling? Almost 90 percent of this country's paper comes from renewable forests, and to say we will someday run out of trees is the same as saying we will some day run out of corn. According to Jerry Taylor, we are growing 22 million acres of new forest each year, and we harvest 15 million acres, for a net annual gain of 7 million acres. The United States has almost four times more forested land today than it did 80 years ago.

Are we running out of that other staple of recycle bins, glass? All those wine and beer bottles are manufactured from silica dioxide, the fancy term for sand, which Jay Lehr points out is the most abundant mineral in the earth's crust.

Nor will we ever suffer a shortage of plastic, which is made from petroleum byproducts. Today more petroleum reserves are being discovered than are being used up. And plastics can now also be synthesized from farm products. Lehr concludes, "We are not running out of, nor will we ever run out of, any of the resources we recycle."

Recycling Has Little or No Reward

Why then do we go to all this trouble for so little—or no—reward? Lehr says it's because "we get a warm and fuzzy feeling when we recycle." Richard Sandbrook who was executive director of the International Institute for Environment and Development, said, "Environmentalists refuse to countenance any argument which undermines their sacred cow."

The *Seattle Times* concludes, "Recycling is almost a religion in Seattle." An irrational religion, says Professor Frank Ackerman, who specializes in environment policy at Tufts University. But his arguments cut little weight here in the Northwest. We attend the church of recycling, where perfervid [exaggeratedly emotional] faith compensates for lack of factual support.

Analyze the essay:

1. James Thayer quotes from several sources to support the points he makes in his essay. Make a list of all the people he quotes, including their credentials and the nature of their comments. Then, analyze his sources: Are they credible? Are they well qualified to speak on this subject?

2. Thayer and Wittbecker (the author of the previous essay) disagree on whether recycling saves or wastes energy. After reading both viewpoints, with which author do you agree? What details helped convince you? Make a list of the top three most persuasive details and what you found compelling about them.

Recycling Should Be Mandatory

Marc Gunther

In the following essay Marc Gunther says that mandatory recycling programs can have a fantastic effect on a city's environment and economy. He describes the mandatory recycling program in San Francisco, California, which has the nation's highest recycling rate. San Francisco makes a lot of money selling recycled materials to manufacturers all over the world. It also enriches the lives of its citizens, who take advantage of high-quality products made from recycled materials. Gunther holds San Francisco up as a model the rest of the country should follow for instituting mandatory recycling programs.

Gunther is a leading thinker, writer, and speaker about business and sustainability.

Consider the following questions:

1. What is San Francisco's recycling rate, according to Gunther?
2. What are the Fantastic Three, as described by Gunther?
3. What is the process for sorting recyclable waste at Norcal facilities, according to the author?

"Garbage," says the character played by Andie MacDowell in [the movie] *Sex, Lies, and Videotape*. "All I've been thinking about all week is garbage. We've got so much of it, you know? I mean, we have to run out of places to put this stuff eventually."

Marc Gunther, "The End of Garbage," *Fortune*, vol. 155, March 19, 2007, pp. 158–166. Copyright © 2007 Time Inc. Reproduced by permission.

In 1989, America had garbage on its mind. A barge called the *Mobro* had carried 3,000 tons of unwanted trash up and down the East Coast. California told its cities to recycle 50% of their garbage by 2000 or face steep fines. The national recycling rate was only 16%.

Leading the Nation in Mandatory Recycling

Today San Francisco has a recycling rate of 68%, the best of any American city, and it intends to do better. Much better. San Francisco and Wal-Mart do not have much in common, but there is this: Both have a goal of achieving zero waste. So do cities and towns from Boulder [Colo.] and Carrboro, N.C., to Buenos Aires [Argentina] and Canberra [Australia], as well as a surprising number of businesses, including Toyota, Nike, and Xerox. They're making headway: Toyota has eliminated all the waste from its 5,000-employee U.S. headquarters near Los Angeles. Governments, meanwhile, are stepping in to regulate the disposal of computers, cellphones, and packaging.

Zero waste is just what it sounds like—producing, consuming, and recycling products without throwing anything away. Getting to a wasteless world will require nothing less than a total makeover of the global economy, which thinkers such as entrepreneur Paul Hawken, consultant Amory Lovins, and architect William McDonough have called the Next Industrial Revolution. They want industry to mimic biology, where one species' excrement is another's food. "We're not talking here about eliminating waste," McDonough explains. "We're talking about eliminating the entire concept of waste."

A New Way to Think About Waste

This utopian vision is a long way off. But the changing economics of waste disposal, technical advances, and grass-roots activism—along with the feverish desire of big companies to appear green—are bringing it closer than you might think.

San Francisco has the toughest recycling law in the nation. Residents are mandated to separate trash, recyclables, and compost or be fined a hundred dollars.

San Francisco offers a glimpse of the future. Norcal Waste Systems, the city's trash hauler, provides customers with color-coded 32-gallon carts known as the Fantastic Three—a blue cart into which they can throw paper, glass, plastics, and metal for recycling; a green cart for food and yard waste; and a black cart that's destined for the landfill. (Remember, in cowboy movies the bad guys wore black.) Norcal also recycles tires, mattresses, and light bulbs. "The other garbage companies think we're nuts," says Mike Sangiacomo, Norcal's CEO.

Sangiacomo, 58, has been trash-talking for years. His dad collected garbage back in the days when sanitation men were called scavengers because they salvaged bottles, rags—"anything they could come up with that had value," he says. Now he's trying to return the waste industry to its roots.

An Innovative System

Technology is a big help. Norcal operates a $38 million facility that disaggregates all the recyclables in those blue bins. Conveyor belts, powerful magnets, and giant vacuums separate computer paper from newsprint, plastic jugs from water bottles, and steel and tin cans from aluminum. Materials are then sold to global commodity markets—and we do mean global. Wastepaper, for example, is the U.S.'s No. 1 export by volume to China, according to PIERS Global Intelligence Solutions, which tracks trade. Ships that bring products from China to the U.S. return with wastepaper, which becomes packaging for goods made in China.

A second innovation is the city's handling of food scraps. Another Norcal facility grinds all that up with yard waste and cures it for three months. Banana peels, onion skins, fish heads, and other detritus are thus transformed into a nutrient-rich product dubbed Four Course Compost, which sells for $8 to $10 per cubic yard.

One satisfied customer is wine-maker Kathleen Inman, who knows that all good wine—her 2004 Olivet Grange pinot noir retails at $42 a bottle—begins in good soil. She spreads Four Course Compost on her ten-acre vineyard in Sonoma County's Russian River Valley. "I was very taken by the concept of bringing into my vineyard what would normally go into a landfill," Inman explains. "When someone enjoys the wine at a table, they are completing the recycling circle."

> ## The Wisdom of Recycling
>
> Most Americans now see the wisdom in banning motorists from tossing paper sacks full of baby diapers on the highway. And using mandatory recycling laws to induce a nudge in the right direction—the direction of accountability and a concern for fellow travelers on Earth—doesn't seem to be demanding the moon.
>
> *Deseret News*, "Make Recycling a Must," September 29, 2008, p. A12.

It Pays to Make Recycling Pay

Driving this virtuous cycle are market incentives. San Franciscans get about $5 off the standard $22-a-month

America's Best and Worst Recyclers

A 2009 study ranked the best and worst American cities for recycling. The rankings are based on issues such as whether recycling is mandatory, how easy it is for residents to recycle, and the percent of households that recycle. Many of the top 10 cities have mandatory recycling programs.

Best

City, State	Ranking
Fresno, CA	1
Fremont,CA	2
San Antonio, TX	3
Burlington, VT	4
Anaheim, CA	5
Pittsburgh, PA	6
Jacksonville, FL	7
San Diego, CA	8
Madison, WI	9
Durham, NC	10

Worst

City, State	Ranking
Louisville, KY	91
Aurora, CO	92
Lincoln, NE	93
Detroit, MI	94
St. Petersburg, FL	95
Lubbock, TX	96
Billings, MT	97
Colorado Springs, CO	98
Las Vegas, NV	99
Wichita, KS	100

Taken from: *Men's Health*, 2009.

collection rate if they can make do with a smaller black bin, sending less to the landfill. Merchants earn discounts for recycling, and Norcal gets bonuses for keeping waste out of landfills. Jared Blumenfeld, director of the city's environment department, says, "The most important thing we do is incentivize people financially to do the right thing and make it more expensive for them to do the wrong thing." This "pay as you throw" pricing scheme drives up recycling rates sharply, studies show. But only about 20% of Americans pay for trash collection based on how much they discard. No wonder we're an effluent society.

While the concept of zero waste is as old as nature, recycling is newer. In 1968, Madison, Wis., became the first U.S. city to offer curbside recycling, for newspapers. Recycling got a boost with Earth Day in 1970, and again after the EPA [Environmental Protection Agency] imposed strict regulations on landfills in 1991. When done right, recycling saves energy, preserves natural resources, reduces greenhouse-gas emissions, and keeps toxins from leaking out of landfills.

Too Much Stuff Is Needlessly Wasted

So why doesn't everyone do it? Because it's often cheaper to throw things away. The economics of recycling depend on landfill fees, the price of oil and other commodities, and the demand for recycled goods. Paper, for example, works well: About 52% of paper consumed in the U.S. is recovered for recycling, and 36% of the fiber that goes into new paper comes from recycled sources. By contrast, less than 25% of plastic bottles are recycled, and we use five billion (!) a year.

Americans generated an average of 4.5 pounds of garbage per person per day in 2005, the EPA reports. About 1.5 pounds were recycled. That's a national recycling rate for municipal solid waste of just 32%.

What's in our garbage? Paper and cardboard (34%), yard trimmings (13%), and food scraps (12%) are the three biggies. All can be easily if not always profitably recycled. Plastics (11.8%) are next, and are harder to recycle. "The plastics industry hasn't been as interested as others in working through its problems," says Gary Liss, a California zero-waste consultant. "They have fought bottle bills all over the country for 30 years."

Bottle bills are an example of "extended producer responsibility," a key tenet of zero-waste. It puts the onus for safely disposing of products on the companies that make them. Yes, it's a controversial concept. (In this country. In the EU, makers of household appliances are obliged to take them back.)

Norcal Waste Systems collects food scraps from two thousand restaurants and thousands of residents to make compost, which it resells to farmers.

"Waste Doesn't Need to Exist"

The deeper purpose here is to change the way things are made. "From our perspective, waste doesn't need to exist," says San Francisco's Blumenfeld. "It's a design flaw." Carpet companies Interface, BASF, and Milliken, furniture makers Herman Miller and Steelcase, and clothing firms Nike and Patagonia have all redesigned products to make them easier to recycle.

Over time the economics of recycling should improve. The costs of virgin commodities are likely to rise as supplies dwindle; fees will climb at landfills as they fill up. Landfills also release methane, a greenhouse gas that could be taxed because it contributes to global warming. Meanwhile, recycling has become a $238 billion business, employing 1.1 million people, according to the EPA.

Analyze the essay:

1. Gunther discusses the concept of "extended producer responsibility." Describe this concept, and then say whether or not you agree with it.

2. Gunther predicts that San Francisco's garbage collection and recycling system will be the future of American trash. What do you think? Will the rest of America adopt San Francisco's recycling system? Why or why not?

Recycling Should Not Be Mandatory

Michael D. Shaw

Recycling should not be required by law argues Michael D. Shaw in the following essay. Shaw believes recycling efforts are more of a trend than a science-based solution for environmental problems. He admits that some recycling programs yield good end-products, but argues there are enough renewable resources and enough space in landfills to avoid recycling. Another reason Shaw thinks recycling should not be mandatory is that manufacturers are voluntarily finding creative ways to turn recycled materials into profitable products without being forced to by the government. In Shaw's opinion, Americans have glorified the role of recycling. He concludes that since voluntary recycling is sufficient, there is no need to require it by law.

Michael D. Shaw is executive vice president and director of marketing for Interscan Corporation, a manufacturer of toxic gas detection instrumentation. He is also a contributing columnist for *Health News Digest*, which covers health, science, and environmental news.

Consider the following questions:

1. According to the author, recycling is like what other fads?
2. For what purpose does Shaw say many trees are specifically grown?
3. Describe the event the author says began the recycling craze. How does it support his argument?

Michael D. Shaw, "Got Waste? The Debate over Recycling," *Health News Digest*, May 23, 2005. Reproduced by permission.

Just how much of what we do every day is based on popular fads or fashion—as opposed to cold, scientific reason? More than most of us would want to admit, I'm afraid.

Recycling Is Just a Fad

The global cooling scare of the 1970's morphed into today's global warming. Breast feeding, presumably a proven commodity over human and mammalian history for millions of years, fell out of favor in the 1950's as not being "modern," and even gross. How many baby boomers were raised on the notion that having meat for at least all three meals, seven days a week, was the only way to build strong American bodies? And, who wasn't indoctrinated into the feel-good notion, raised to a religious precept by some, that recycling is the cornerstone of any waste management program, and must be practiced by all people all the time?

Cities can encourage residents to recycle without force. A reminder could be as simple as placing encouraging signs throughout local areas.

It was nine years ago [1996] that John Tierney's land-mark article, entitled "Recycling Is Garbage" appeared in the *New York Times Magazine*. Focusing primarily on recycling efforts in New York City, he exposed the high expenses in collecting and separating the garbage, and the lack of demand for most of the resulting materials. Moreover, in some cases, such as recycling newspaper, more water pollution ensues (owing to removing the ink), than in making new paper. Besides, trees are specifically grown for this purpose, and are a renewable resource.

He also reassured the public on landfill site availability, noting that if Americans keep generating garbage at current rates for the next 1,000 years, and if all this refuse is put in a landfill 100 yards deep, by the year

Opponents of mandating recycling say it will increase the number of trucks that consume fossil fuels and cause air pollution.

3000, this accumulation of trash will fill a plot of land 35 miles on each side. This area, by the way, is about 5 percent the size of the space needed for solar panels, as touted by various environmental groups.

Recycling's Roots

So, what's the big deal? Would it surprise you that the incident behind the hysteria over landfills, the infamous 1987 voyage of the barge *Mobro 4000*, containing 3,168 tons of Long Island trash, is a complete travesty? Chartered by entrepreneur Lowell Harrelson and Long Island mob boss Salvatore Avellino, the craft was headed for a pilot program in Morehead City, North Carolina to be turned into methane. But, before the barge reached its destination, a rumor began to circulate (never verified and most likely untrue) that the load contained medical waste. At that, the permits to unload were denied, and it continued to travel south, facing military force in Mexico, before finally arriving at a Brooklyn incinerator five months later.

> ### Recycling Does Not Solve the Garbage Problem
>
> We obsess over recycling, demand that our cities make it cost neutral and effortless, yet at the same time, we discard "garbage" with impunity. Recycling gives us permission to consume. But putting a week's worth of plastic bottles into a clear bag instead of a black one doesn't address the real problem.
>
> Bill McKibben, "Recycling? Fuhgeddaboudit: Are New Yorkers Right to Think Recycling Is a Waste of Time?" *Mother Jones*, May–June 2009, pp. 52–55.

Thus, given the bad publicity of mob ties and a vicious rumor, the recycling craze was born. Ironically, there never was a problem with finding a Long Island landfill. The whole thing occurred because Harrelson was trying to beat the high tipping fees of the local facilities, and assure himself of a big profit.

Tierney made many other strong points in his article, including a defense of Styrofoam coffee cups and the amount of waste at fast food restaurants. But, save a quick rebuttal from the Environmental Defense Fund (EDF), few voices were raised in opposition to his startlingly contrarian piece. As it was, the EDF essay contained numerous examples of classical fallacies in logic, and must have been embarrassing to even the group's most ardent supporters.

Voluntary Recycling Works

Are there any good news recycling stories? Certainly. Aluminum recycling is one of the original triumphs. Glass waste has been used in the production of new glass for decades. Engineered wood products, melding sawmill waste with newly harvested forest products, offer advantages over conventional goods in price, strength, and durability.

There is also an active market in plastics recycling. Poly-Wood, Inc. transforms milk jugs, once destined for landfills, into recycled plastic lumber used to create a pleasing line of casual outdoor furniture. For my money, it beats wicker and wood hands down. Recycline manufactures a range of personal care items, all from recycled plastic. The company also supplies postpaid mailers, for return of the products, into their destiny as plastic lumber.

Recycling Is Not the Holy Grail

Plastic, far from being an environmental villain, as it has been portrayed, is proving itself to be highly recyclable, into products people actually want to buy. This should come as no surprise, since regrinding of plastic molding waste, for all applications except those that require clarity, is standard procedure. And, while paper is more biodegradable than plastic, this, too is a false issue, since in the low oxygen environment of landfills, neither paper nor plastic break down all that much. Another fad shattered?

Recycling surely has its place, and its role is growing, but it is not the holy grail. And, neither is technology the enemy, for without it, there would be scant time for environmental reason, or environmental reverie, for that matter.

Analyze the essay:

1. In this essay, Shaw uses history, facts, and examples to make his argument that the United States does not need recycling laws. He does not, however, use any quotations to support his point. If you were to rewrite this article and insert quotations, what authorities might you quote from? Where would you place these quotations to bolster the points Shaw makes?

2. Investigate whether your school or community has mandatory recycling laws. Write a short report on what these laws are, and whether you agree with them. If your school or community has no such laws, write an essay either advocating for their institution or arguing why they are not necessary. Use the points both Shaw and Gunther make in their essays to jumpstart your thinking on the matter.

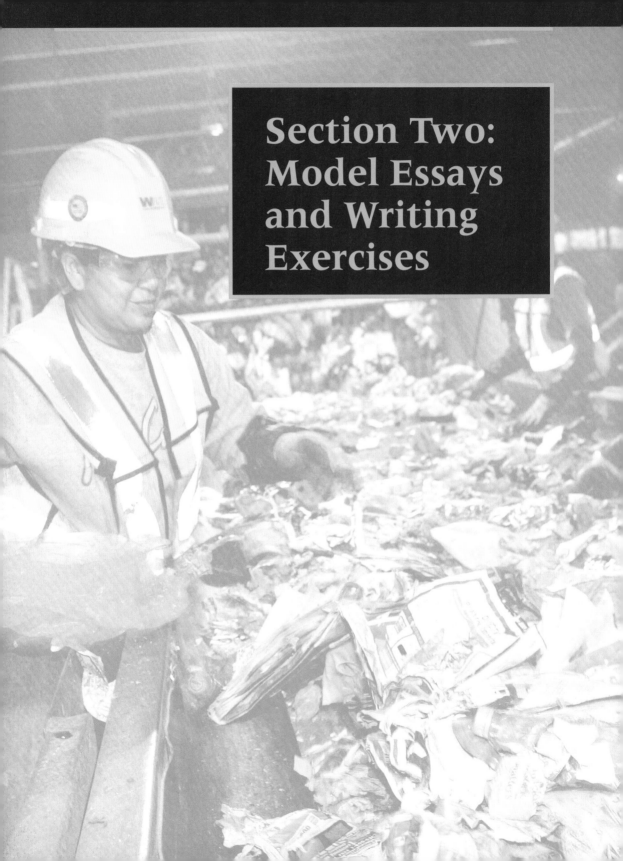

Section Two: Model Essays and Writing Exercises

The Five-Paragraph Essay

An *essay* is a short piece of writing that discusses or analyzes one topic. The five-paragraph essay is a form commonly used in school assignments and tests. Every five-paragraph essay begins with an *introduction*, ends with a *conclusion*, and features three *supporting paragraphs* in the middle.

The Thesis Statement. The introduction includes the essay's thesis statement. The thesis statement presents the argument or point the author is trying to make about the topic. The essays in this book all have different thesis statements because they are making different arguments about recycling.

The thesis statement should clearly tell the reader what the essay will be about. A focused thesis statement helps determine what will be in the essay; the subsequent paragraphs are spent developing and supporting its argument.

The Introduction. In addition to presenting the thesis statement, a well-written introductory paragraph captures the attention of the reader and explains why the topic being explored is important. It may provide the reader with background information on the subject matter or feature an anecdote that illustrates a point relevant to the topic. It could also present startling information that clarifies the point of the essay or put forth a contradictory position that the essay will refute. Further techniques for writing an introduction are found later in this section.

The Supporting Paragraphs. The introduction is then followed by three (or more) supporting paragraphs. These are the main body of the essay. Each paragraph presents and develops a *subtopic* that supports the essay's thesis statement. Each subtopic is spearheaded by a *topic*

55

sentence and supported by its own facts, details, and examples. The writer can use various kinds of supporting material and details to back up the topic of each supporting paragraph. These may include statistics, quotations from people with special knowledge or expertise, historic facts, and anecdotes. A rule of writing is that specific and concrete examples are more convincing than vague, general, or unsupported assertions.

The Conclusion. The conclusion is the paragraph that closes the essay. Its function is to summarize or reiterate the main idea of the essay. It may recall an idea from the introduction or briefly examine the larger implications of the thesis. Because the conclusion is also the last chance a writer has to make an impression on the reader, it is important that it not simply repeat what has been presented elsewhere in the essay but close it in a clear, final, and memorable way.

Although the order of the essay's component paragraphs is important, they do not have to be written in the order presented here. Some writers like to decide on a thesis and write the introduction paragraph first. Other writers like to focus first on the body of the essay, and write the introduction and conclusion later.

Pitfalls to Avoid

When writing essays about controversial issues such as recycling, it is important to remember that disputes over the material are common precisely because there are many different perspectives. Remember to state your arguments in careful and measured terms. Evaluate your topic fairly—avoid overstating negative qualities of one perspective or understating positive qualities of another. Use examples, facts, and details to support any assertions you make.

The Descriptive Essay

The previous section of this book provided you with samples of published persuasive writing on recycling. Many of these essays used description to convey their message. In this section you will focus on developing your own descriptive writing skills.

A descriptive essay gives a reader a mental picture of the subject that the writer is exploring. Typically, descriptive writing uses the five senses—sight, sound, touch, taste, and smell—to help the reader experience what the writer has experienced. A descriptive writer carefully selects vivid examples and specific details to reveal people, places, processes, events, and ideas.

Using the Descriptive Essay

While an essay can be purely descriptive, descriptive papers written for the classroom are often persuasive or expository essays that use description to explain a memory, discuss an experience, or make a point. For example, in Viewpoint Four, James Thayer argues that Americans' image of landfills is outdated and inaccurate. But rather than simply say this, he describes the Fresh Kills landfill in Staten Island, saying that when Americans think of it, they picture "a vast swampy expanse of detritus, with huge Caterpillar tractors trundling over it, and clouds of seagulls obscuring everything above ground." The specific details he includes give the reader concrete and vivid images and help the author drive home his point that modern landfills are no longer like this.

Sometimes descriptive essays are written in the first person (from the "I" point of view). Descriptive essays are a good format for the first person because details about a particular event or experience are well delivered through a person's memories, experiences, or opinions.

Descriptive Writing Techniques

An important element of descriptive writing is the use of images and specific and concrete details. "Specific and concrete" is the opposite of "general and abstract." Descriptive writers should give their readers a fuller understanding of the topic by focusing on tangible details and by appealing to the five senses. See the accompanying box for examples of general nouns and their more specific variations.

General and Specific Descriptions

General	More specific	Most specific
vegetation	trees	maple
animal	fish	shark
grocery item	breakfast food	omelet
sound	crash	car accident

The use of *metaphors* and *similes* can also enliven descriptive writing. A *metaphor* is a word or phrase that compares two objects. A simile is a metaphor that includes the prepositions *like* or *as*.

Some descriptive essays make use of *scene* and *exposition*. The *scene* is an element commonly found in fiction and in creative writing. With scene, a writer describes an event with moment-by-moment detail, often including dialogue if people are involved. With *exposition,* a writer explains, summarizes, or concisely recounts events that occur between scenes. Scene is comparable to "showing," while exposition is similar to "telling."

Tips to Remember

A descriptive essay should give the reader a clear impression of its subject. So, a writer must select the most relevant details. A few well-chosen details are more effective than dozens of random ones. You want the reader to visualize what you are describing but not feel overloaded with information. The room you are sitting in now, for example, is likely full of many concrete and specific items. To describe the room in writing, however, you would want to choose just a few of the most vivid details that would help convey your impression of and attitude about it.

A writer should also be aware of the kinds of words he or she uses in descriptive passages. Modifying words like adjectives and adverbs can enhance descriptive writing, but they should be used sparingly. Generally, verbs and nouns are more powerful than adjectives and adverbs. The overuse of modifying words makes the writing seem "wordy" and unnatural. Compare the phrases in the accompanying box to see the difference between wordy and concise language.

Wordy vs. Concise Language

Wordy	Concise
bright green potted plant with thin leaves	fern
rolling around rapidly in brilliant untamed magnificence	dancing in wild splendor
she stopped extremely abruptly	she stopped
the best most amazingly wonderful experience	a fantastic time

In the rest of this section you will read model descriptive essays about recycling and work on exercises that will help you write your own.

Recycling Is Ineffective

**Refers to thesis
and topic
sentences**

**Refers to
supporting
details**

Editor's Notes The first model essay argues against recycling efforts. It is structured as a five-paragraph descriptive essay in which each paragraph contributes a distinct supporting idea that develops the argument. The author uses descriptive and persuasive techniques to convince the reader that recycling wastes energy, money, and resources.

The notes in the margin point out key features of the essay and will help you understand how the essay is organized. Also note that all sources are cited using Modern Language Association (MLA) style.* For more information on how to cite your sources see Appendix C. In addition, consider the following:

1. How does the introduction engage the reader's attention?
2. What descriptive techniques are used in the essay?
3. What purpose do the essay's quotes serve?
4. Does the essay convince you of its point?

Paragraph 1

The essay begins with specific, descriptive details meant to grab your attention.

The image of a scrubbed, label-free tin can ready for the recycling bin is one many Americans have come to feel good about. By sticking their rinsed yogurt containers, empty water bottles, and shiny glass jars into large bins with the familiar triangular recycling logo on the side, they feel satisfied in thinking they have helped save the planet in a gesture that took less than ten seconds. But in reality, recycling is a feel-good environmental measure only. It offers little in the way of environmental usefulness and often wastes more resources than it conserves.

* Editor's Note: In applying MLA style guidelines in this book, the following simplifications have been made: Parenthetical text citations are confined to direct quotations only; electronic source documentation in the Works Cited list omits date of access, page ranges, and some detailed facts of publication.

A closer look at recycling reveals that it wastes energy, is expensive, and uselessly conserves resources that are already in abundance.

Paragraph 2

Although recycling is billed as an energy-saving measure, in reality it expends more energy than it is worth. In Los Angeles, for example, recycling programs require that four hundred additional trucks drive around the city each day to pick up garbage destined for recycling centers. Those trucks are powered by gas, which is an expensive and dwindling energy source. Furthermore, the burning of fossil fuels emits harmful climate-change-causing gases into the atmosphere when burned. "Recycling requires twice as many trucks, twice as much gas consumption, and thus twice as much atmospheric pollution," says one observer (McMillan). Even more energy is expended when plastic, aluminum, glass, and paper are sorted and processed for recycling.

Paragraph 3

Recycling is also wasteful when it costs communities thousands of dollars more than sending garbage to a landfill. According to professor Daniel K. Benjamin, who is a senior fellow at PERC, the Property and Environment Research Center, curbside recycling programs—which are among the most utilized where available since people do not have to drive to recycling centers on their own—costs between 35 and 55 percent more than if the trash were to be simply disposed of in a landfill. In New York City, for example, it costs $240 to recycle a ton of garbage but only $130 to send that same ton of garbage to a landfill. In Rhode Island, recycling costs more than $180 per ton, while normal trash collection costs about $120–$160 per ton. This is why Jay Lehr, science director of the Heartland Institute, has said, "Every community recycling program in America today costs more than the revenue it generates" (qtd. in Thayer). With such a high price tag, recycling wastes communities' valuable economic resources while not offering them very much in return.

This is the essay's thesis statement. It tells the reader what will be argued in the following paragraphs.

This is the topic sentence of Paragraph 2. It is a subset of the essay's thesis.

This is a *supporting detail*. This information directly supports the topic sentence, helping to prove it true.

This quote was taken from the quote box that accompanies Viewpoint Two. When you see particularly striking quotes, save them to use to support points in your essays.

This is the topic sentence of Paragraph 3. It argues a different aspect of the essay's thesis. Note that all of the paragraph's details fit with it—or, *support* it.

These details were taken from Viewpoint Four in this book. Get in the habit of using information from credible sources to support arguments made in your essays.

What is the topic sentence of Paragraph 4? How did you recognize it?

Paragraph 4

Finally, most of the products that get recycled are not in danger of being depleted, which makes recycling appear to be an even more useless endeavor. The most common waste products that get recycled are paper, glass, and plastic. But all three of these products are made from resources that are abundant and do not need to be conserved. Most paper is made from renewable forests, which are planted expressly for the purpose of manufacturing paper. Most glass is made from a derivative of sand, which is in about as short supply as salt water. Finally, plastic is made from petroleum by-products, many of which are increasingly being made synthetically. As Lehr says, "We are not running out of, nor will we ever run out of, any of the resources we recycle" (qtd. in Thayer). One has to wonder, then: Why are we spending so much money and wasting so much energy in recycling resources that exist in great abundance?

Note how this quote supports the ideas discussed in the paragraph. It also comes from a reputable source.

Paragraph 5

Although Americans have been trained to view recycling as the be-all and end-all of environmental gestures, in reality recycling wastes energy, is expensive, and conserves resources that are widely available. For all of these reasons, the environmental usefulness of recycling should be reconsidered. Though it has been hailed as an environmental fix-all, recycling efforts are not the most effective or efficient way to solve the serious environmental problems we face.

Note how the author returns to ideas introduced in Paragraph 1. See Exercise 2A for more on introductions and conclusions.

Works Cited

McMillan, Lucas. "Recycling's Myth: The 'Three R's' Are Doing More Harm than Good." *Times-Delphic* [Drake University] 19 Nov. 2007.

Thayer, James. "Recycle This! Separating Tin Cans and Pizza Boxes and Exposing the Facts About the High Church of Recycling." *Weekly Standard* 26 Jan. 2006.

Exercise 1A: Create an Outline from an Existing Essay

It often helps to create an outline of the five-paragraph essay before you write it. The outline can help you organize the information, arguments, and evidence you have gathered during your research.

For this exercise, create an outline that could have been used to write "Recycling Is Ineffective." This "reverse engineering" exercise is meant to help familiarize you with how outlines can help classify and arrange information.

To do this you will need to

1.   articulate the essay's thesis,
2.   pinpoint important pieces of evidence,
3.   flag quotes that supported the essay's ideas, and
4.   identify key points that supported the argument.

Part of the outline has already been started to give you an idea of the assignment.

Outline

I. Paragraph One
Write the essay's thesis: Recycling wastes energy, is expensive, and helps conserve resources that are already in abundance.

II. Paragraph Two
Topic:

Supporting Detail i.

Supporting Detail ii. Quote from Lucas McMillan: "Recycling requires twice as many trucks, twice as much gas consumption, and thus twice as much atmospheric pollution."

III. Paragraph Three
Topic: Recycling is expensive.

Supporting Detail i. It costs between 35 and 55 percent more to recycle trash than to simply dispose of it in a landfill.

Supporting Detail ii.

IV. Paragraph Four
Topic:

Supporting Detail i.

Supporting Detail ii. Quote from Jay Lehr that supports the idea that recycled items are not in danger of running out: "We are not running out of, nor will we ever run out of, any of the resources we recycle."

V. Paragraph Five
Write the essay's conclusion:

Exercise 1B: Create an Outline for Your Own Essay

The first model essay makes a particular argument about recycling. For this exercise, your assignment is to find supporting ideas, choose specific and concrete details, create an outline, and ultimately write your own five-paragraph essay about recycling. Your goal is to use descriptive techniques to convince your reader.

Part I: Write a thesis statement.

The following thesis statement would be appropriate for an essay on why recycling is effective:

When done properly, recycling saves enormous amounts of energy and prevents industry from needing to make new products out of raw materials.

The following essay would then explore reasons that this statement is true. If you would like to pick a different topic, see the sample paper topics suggested in Appendix D for more ideas.

Part II: Brainstorm pieces of supporting evidence.

Using information found in this book and from your own research, write down three arguments or pieces of evidence that support the thesis statement you selected. Then, for each of these three arguments, write down supportive facts, examples, and details that support it. These could be:

- statistical information;
- personal memories and anecdotes;
- quotes from experts, peers, or family members;
- observations of people's actions and behaviors;
- specific and concrete details.

Supporting pieces of evidence for the above sample thesis statement include:

- Fact from Viewpoint One by Tom Zeller Jr. about how 83 percent of the time, recycling is better for the environment than burying or burning waste.
- Fact from Viewpoint Two by Rachel Cernansky about how it takes two-thirds less energy to make products from recycled plastic than from new plastic, and how recycling efforts save as much greenhouse gas from entering the atmosphere as would taking 39.6 million cars off the road.

- Quote from Viewpoint Three by Greg Wittbecker: "Recycling a ton of aluminum uses just 5 percent of the energy required to make virgin metal." This quote could be used to support the argument that recycling saves energy.
- Chart accompanying Viewpoint Three that shows the energy savings from recycled materials.

Part III: Place the information from Part I in outline form.

Part IV: Write the arguments or supporting statements in paragraph form.

By now you have three arguments that support the essay's thesis statement, as well as supporting material. Use the outline to write out your three supporting arguments in paragraph form. Make sure each paragraph has a topic sentence that states the paragraph's thesis clearly and broadly. Then, add supporting sentences that express the facts, quotes, details, and examples that support the paragraph's argument. The paragraph may also have a concluding or summary sentence.

The Wisdom of Toilet-to-Tap

Editor's Notes The following model essay argues that wastewater recycling programs should be used in cities that are facing severe droughts. Like the first model essay, this essay is structured as a five-paragraph descriptive essay in which each paragraph contributes a supporting piece of evidence to develop the argument. Each supporting paragraph explores one of three distinct reasons why the author thinks that recycling wastewater should be initiated in drought-stricken American cities.

As you did for the first model essay, take note of the essay's components and how they are organized (the sidebars in the margins will help you identify the essay's pieces and their purpose).

Refers to thesis and topic sentences

Refers to supporting details

Paragraph 1

It is a hot, sunny day, and you are parched. You reach for a nice refreshing glass of ... toilet water? Could it be true? It sounds unfathomable, but toilet-to-tap initiatives—the off-putting nickname of projects that filter, purify, and recycle wastewater for other purposes—are becoming a reality in drought-stricken areas of the United States. Because the thought of drinking recycled sewage is unappealing, such programs are controversial in regions where they have been proposed. But despite their unpleasant association, such programs hold great promise for providing clean water to otherwise struggling areas.

Look at Exercise 2B on introductions. What type of introduction is this? Does it grab your attention?

What is the essay thesis statement?

Paragraph 2

Toilet-to-tap programs work, and an example of a successful one was launched in 2008 in Orange County, California. There, sewage water is taken straight from residential bathrooms. It is given an initial cleansing treatment in which solid waste is removed and microorganisms are used to break down organic waste particles. The water

This is the topic sentence of Paragraph 2. Without reading the rest of the paragraph, guess what the paragraph will be about.

67

is then sent through a 490-million-dollar purification system of pipes, filters, and tanks that strain out particulate matter, bacteria, single-celled organisms, viruses, salts, and pesticides. It is then treated with hydrogen peroxide and ultraviolet light to further clean it. Next, the water is transported to outdoor lakes, where it is filtered through clay, sand, and rock before making its way to natural underground aquifers the same way rainwater would. Eventually it is recollected and piped back into the showerheads, sinks, and kitchen taps of county residents' homes.

> The details in this paragraph describe a process. When describing a process, you need to use specific, concrete details that make clear to your reader all the elements of the process.

Paragraph 3

This system is very efficient at purifying water that comes out more than clean enough to drink. In fact, treated wastewater meets or even exceeds the cleanliness of water that is already coming out of taps in cities such as San Diego (where a multi-year drought has made water scarce and toilet-to-tap programs could provide residents with much relief). Robert Bastian, an environmental scientist with the Environmental Protection Agency, says that with such treatment programs, "you're getting even better tracking of the quality of the . . . water than you would if it were coming from more 'natural' sources. You know more about the water that's recharging the area now because you have control of it all the way" (qtd. in Barone). No one denies that somewhat of an "ick" factor is associated with recycled water programs. As one reporter, Eilene Zimmerman, put it, "A majority of us don't want to drink water that once had poop in it, even if it's been cleaned and purified" (Zimmerman). However, Zimmerman and others agree that since the treated water ends up more than clean enough to drink, such programs should be implemented.

> What is the topic sentence of Paragraph 3? How did you recognize it?

> Why do you think the author has included Robert Bastian's job title?

> Analyze this quote. Why do you think the author selected it for inclusion in the essay?

Paragraph 4

Toilet-to-tap programs could make an enormous difference in communities that are struggling to meet their water needs. San Diego, for example, is experiencing

> "For example" is a transitional phrase that keeps the ideas in the essay flowing. Make a list of all transitional words and phrases used in the essay.

a severe water crisis: The city imports 90 percent of its water from a delta in northern California and the Colorado River, both of which are drying up. As of 2009 San Diego had only enough water for 10 percent of its residents and had imposed water rationing restrictions in an attempt to save every precious drop. San Diegans and residents of other drought-stricken cities such as Phoenix, Arizona, would do well to consider that the Orange County treatment system creates 70 million gallons of clean water a day, water that would have otherwise been dumped into the Pacific Ocean. Seventy million gallons a day could go a long way for residents in communities wondering where their next shower or drink might come from.

What point in Paragraph 4 does this detail directly support?

Paragraph 5

Recycled water projects are not new. For decades, American cities have used recycled wastewater for agriculture and landscaping. But now technology exists to purify this water so that it is clean enough to drink, a breakthrough that can make a major difference in meeting the needs of people who live in places where water is becoming scarcer. Because water is one of our most precious—and finite—resources, not a drop should be wasted. Toilet-to-tap programs are like knights in shining armor that can save many cities from crisis and shortfall. Americans would do well to throw off the stigma attached to toilet-to-tap programs—instead, they should grab a glass and drink up.

The author uses a simile to drive home her argument that toilet-to-tap programs are useful. For more on similes and other descriptive techniques see Preface B.

Works Cited

Barone, Jennifer. "From Toilet to Tap: Filtered Sewage Water May Be the Key Water Source of the 21st Century." *Discover* May 2008.

Zimmerman, Eilene. "It's Time to Drink Toilet Water: Recycling Sewage Is Safe and Efficient, So Why Aren't We Doing it?" Slate.com 25 Jan. 2008 <www.slate.com/id/2182758>.

Exercise 2A: Create an Outline from an Existing Essay

As you did for the first model essay in this section, create an outline that could have been used to write "The Wisdom of Toilet-to-Tap." Be sure to identify the essay's thesis statement, its supporting ideas and details, and key pieces of evidence that were used.

Exercise 2B: Examining Introductions and Conclusions

Whether an essay is a first-person account, an objective profile, or a formal persuasive paper, all pieces of writing feature introductory and concluding paragraphs that are used to frame the main ideas being presented. Along with presenting the essay's thesis statement, well-written introductions should grab the attention of the reader and make clear why the topic being explored is important. The conclusion reiterates the essay's thesis and is also the last chance for the writer to make an impression on the reader. Strong introductions and conclusions can greatly enhance an essay's effect on an audience.

The Introduction
There are several techniques that can be used to craft an introductory paragraph. An essay can start with:

- an anecdote: a brief story that illustrates a point relevant to the topic;
- startling information: facts, statistics, or shocking descriptive information that elucidates the point of the essay;
- setting up and knocking down a position: a position or claim believed by proponents of one side of a controversy, followed by statements that challenge that claim;
- historical perspective: an example of the way things used to be that leads into a discussion of how or why things work differently now;

- summary information: general introductory information about the topic that feeds into the essay's thesis statement.

Problem One
Reread the introductory paragraphs of the model essays and of the viewpoints in Section One. Identify which of the techniques described above are used in the example essays. How do they grab the attention of the reader? Are their thesis statements clearly presented?

Problem Two
Write an introduction for the essay you have outlined and partially written in Exercise 1B, using one of the techniques described above.

The Conclusion
The conclusion brings the essay to a close by summarizing or returning to its main ideas. Good conclusions, however, go beyond simply repeating these ideas. Strong conclusions explore a topic's broader implications and reiterate why it is important to consider. They may frame the essay by returning to an anecdote featured in the opening paragraph. Or they may close with a quotation or refer back to an event in the essay. In opinionated essays, the conclusion can reiterate which side the essay is taking or ask the reader to reconsider a previously held position on the subject.

Problem Three
Reread the concluding paragraphs of the model essays and of the viewpoints in Section One. Which were most effective in driving their arguments home to the reader? What sorts of techniques did they use to do this? Did they appeal emotionally to the reader or bookend an idea or event referenced elsewhere in the essay?

Problem Four
Write a conclusion for the essay you have outlined and partially written in Exercise 1B using one of the techniques described above.

Exercise 2C: Using Quotations to Enliven Your Essay

No essay is complete without quotations. Get in the habit of using quotes to support at least some of the ideas in your essays. Quotes do not need to appear in every paragraph, but often enough so that the essay contains voices aside from your own. When you write, use quotations to accomplish the following:

- Provide expert advice that you are not necessarily in the position to know about.
- Cite lively or passionate passages.
- Include a particularly well-written point that gets to the heart of the matter.
- Supply statistics or facts that have been derived from someone's research.
- Deliver anecdotes that illustrate the point you are trying to make.
- Express first-person testimony.

Problem One
Reread the essays presented in all sections of this book and find at least one example of each of the above quotation types.

There are a couple of important things to remember when using quotations.

- Note your sources' qualifications and biases. This way your reader can identify the person you have quoted and can put their words in a context.
- Put any quoted material within proper quotation marks. Failing to attribute quotes to their authors constitutes plagiarism, which is an author taking someone else's words or ideas and presenting them as his or her own. Plagiarism is a very serious infraction and must be avoided at all costs.

Students Seek Recycling on Campus

Editor's Notes The third model essay discusses recycling using a different aspect of the descriptive essay. It reports on a student-led effort to get recycling instituted at a California high school. It uses descriptive techniques to capture the details of the effort, helping the students' efforts come alive for the reader. To do this, the author conducted an interview with the organizer of the effort, Navarro Ellister,* and others who were involved. The information gleaned during the course of the interviews allowed the author to get inside information, details, and opinions on the event. Because they yield these types of details, interviews can be a useful tool when writing a descriptive essay. More information about conducting an interview is found in Exercises 3A and 3B that follow the essay.

Also, unlike the previous model essays, the following essay has more than five paragraphs. Sometimes five paragraphs are simply not enough to adequately develop an idea. Extending the length of an essay can allow the reader to explore a topic in more depth or present multiple pieces of evidence that together provide a complete picture of a topic. Longer essays can also help readers discover the complexity of a subject by examining a topic beyond its superficial exterior. Moreover, the ability to write a sustained research or position paper is a valuable skill you will need as you advance academically.

■ Refers to thesis and topic sentences

■ Refers to supporting details

Paragraph 1

In 2009 a group of motivated students at an Oakland, California, high school started a grassroots effort to bring recycling services to their school. According to seventeen-year-old Navarro Ellister who led the effort, "A bunch of

*Name has been changed to protect Ellister's privacy.

73

These comments lend the essay a personal feel. Make sure to integrate unique and interesting quotes from those you have interviewed.

us were tired of seeing plastic water bottles, Styrofoam, and Coke cans end up in the trash after lunch every day. As a center of learning, we're supposed to be progressive. And recycling is a basic environmental activity that everyone should be participating in." Their experience serves as an inspiring template for all students interested in becoming active about the environment and school policy.

Paragraph 2

Ellister was moved to organize the effort to get recycling on campus after researching the issue for a project in his social studies class. He was asked to write a paper outlining the pros and cons of recycling, and he came to the conclusion that recycling saves energy, saves resources, generates business, and is therefore worth doing. "It's such a simple activity that can have very extended benefits for our planet," he said.

Paragraph 3

Ellister knew he would need help in changing the way his school viewed trash, and so he decided to form a group dedicated to starting a recycling program on campus. He called the group "Waste Not!" As per school policy, he needed a teacher to sponsor the group. After finding one, he hung flyers around school asking fellow classmates who felt passionately about the issue to join. About twenty students came to the first meeting. "At first I thought the only people who would join would be hippie-types," said Ellister, "but it was a total mix of all different types of students—the common thread was that we all think we have a responsibility to do what we can to protect the Earth."

Note how these specific details give you a very clear idea of how Ellister went about pursuing his goal.

Paragraph 4

At the group's first meeting, they articulated their goal: to convince their school, and most importantly, the school's administrators that a recycling program should be adopted. They then debated ways to make this goal a reality. Activities that needed to be accomplished included researching the cost of bringing a recycling program to the school, contracting recycling vendors and getting bids from them, conducting a public relations campaign that would convince the student body and the administrators that the extra costs were worth it, and meeting with various representatives from the school and city who could make the effort come to fruition.

What descriptive details are found in Paragraph 4? What specific information is provided?

Paragraph 5

Once they adopted a plan of action, "Waste Not!" members broke into subgroups to research the issue and handle the various responsibilities. Students who were comfortable writing were placed in charge of submitting articles about the effort to the school paper. They also penned persuasive letters to school administrators letting them know of the effort and why they should favor it. Students who liked to work online were tasked with creating a Web site for the effort. The site featured a blog of ongoing activities and news about the group's activities. Other students were put in charge of circulating a petition around the student body so the group could show widespread support for the endeavor.

What is the topic sentence of Paragraph 5? How did you recognize it?

Paragraph 6

Once they raised awareness about their intentions to get recycling on campus, the group decided to hold a one-day environment fair that would feature all the reasons they wanted recycling to be available on campus. First, they obtained permission from school authorities to hold the event. This included getting the appropriate signatures on permissions forms, finding a school space that was not otherwise occupied on the day they wanted to hold the event, and getting the school's custodial and technology teams to help them rent tables, chairs, podiums, projectors, laptops, and other equipment, and to clean up before and after the event.

Paragraph 7

On the day of the fair, the students set up booths at which their peers could get information on why recycling is important. Each booth featured elaborate graphs and charts that showed the energy savings from recycled materials, such as a ton of paper or aluminum. Students printed up bulleted fact sheets about the energy and resource savings offered by recycling. They also ran demonstrations about what types of trash can be put into recycling bins and what types of trash should be reserved for garbage. Said one participating student, "Even if the effort wasn't going to get adopted, we wanted people to be able to take what they learned about recycling and practice it at home." The fair was a success in that more than half the student body showed up and were exposed to the group's message.

Paragraph 8

But "Waste Not!" faced one final hurdle in getting school officials to adopt the recycling effort: to convince them that recycling would not be too expensive and, in some ways, might save the school money. "Right now, it costs our school about $100 to throw away each ton of trash," said Ellister. "To add recycling to the program, it would cost another $80 per ton. Though that seems like a lot more, when you break it down it works out to just pennies per student, which is a minor cost." Furthermore, Ellister's group pointed out to officials that recycling water bottles, soda cans, plastic containers, tin foil, milk cartons, and other common items would take them out of the regular trash stream, reducing the size and weight of the school's overall trash output. This would mean the school could potentially save money because they would be paying for less garbage to be hauled away. "The savings can then be put towards the recycling costs," reasoned Ellister.

Note how the author obtained a quote that perfectly supports the paragraph's topic sentence.

Paragraph 9

Ultimately, the effort to bring recycling to campus was successful. By the beginning of the following semester, school officials agreed to adopt an on-campus recycling program. They used the research conducted by the students to entertain bids from local haulers and selected a recycling company with which to partner on the effort. Blue recycle bins were displayed in all campus cafeterias and next to highly trafficked trash cans that surround the school. "Waste Not!" members agreed to help custodial staff drag the bins to the back of the school twice a month on collection days to make recycling pickup easier and less expensive. Said Ellister, "I couldn't have asked for a better outcome. Our hard work really paid off, and now recycling on campus is a reality. This is a great example of the ways in which students can positively impact their schools, community, and the planet itself."

Paragraph 10

Ellister and his peers are one of many examples of how American students have successfully brought recycling programs to their campuses. For more information on recycling or for tips on how to start a recycling program at your school, check out RecycleWorks School Recycling Programs. They can be reached online at www.recycleworks.org/schools/schoolpgm.html or via phone at (650) 599-1424. They offer step-by-step instructions for getting a recycling program started on school and college campuses.

> When writing a report, it is a good idea to let your readers know where they can find more information on the event or subject.

Works Cited

Friedman, Lauri S. Interviews 31 Oct. 2009.

Exercise 3A: Conducting an Interview

Model Essay Three, "Students Seek Recycling on Campus," was written after conducting interviews with Navarro Ellister and several other people. When reporting on events that occur in your community, you will probably need to interview people to get critical information and opinions. Interviews allow you to get the story behind a participant's experiences, enabling you to provide a fuller picture of the event.

The key to a successful interview is asking the right questions. You want the respondent to answer in as much detail as possible so you can write an accurate, colorful, and interesting piece. Therefore, you should have a clear idea of what general pieces of information you want to find out from the respondent before you begin interviewing. The five classic journalist questions—who, what, when, where, why—and how—are an excellent place to begin. If you get answers to each of these questions, you will end up with a pretty good picture of the event that took place.

There are many ways to conduct an interview, but the following suggestions will help you get started:

Step One: Choose a setting with little distraction.

Avoid bright lights or loud noises, and make sure the person you are interviewing feels comfortable speaking to you. Professional settings such as offices, places of business, and homes are always appropriate settings for an interview. If it is a phone interview, be sure you can clearly hear what the person is saying (so do not conduct the interview on a cell phone while walking on a busy city block, for example).

Step Two: Explain who you are and what you intend to learn from the interview.

Identify yourself. For what publication are you writing? If you are writing for a school paper, identify the paper.

If you are conducting research for an ongoing project, explain the project's goals and in what way you expect the interviewee can help you reach them. Indicate how long you expect the interview to take, and get all contact information upfront.

Step Three: Ask specific questions, and start at the beginning.

Make sure you ask at least two questions that address each of the following ideas: who, what, where, when, why, and how. Who was involved in the event? What happened during the course of the event? Where did it take place? Specific questions will change depending on what type of event you are covering. Follow your instincts; if you do not know something or have a question, ask. The answer will likely yield good information that will enhance your report.

Step Four: Take notes.

Never rely on your memory when conducting an interview. Either type or jot down notes, or ask permission to tape or otherwise record the interview.

Step Five: Verify quotes and information.

Before you write your report, it is important to go back to your source to double-check key points of information. Also, you must run by the source any quotes you intend to use before you put them in your report. This is to make sure you heard the person accurately and are not misrepresenting their position.

Types of Questions to Ask During an Interview

Questions you will ask your interviewee tend to fall into a few basic categories:

Knowledge—What he or she knows about the topic or event. This can include historical background, logistics, and outcomes of an event. For example, Navarro Ellister in Model Essay Three provided the interviewer with information about the process of getting a recycling program adopted at his school.

Sensory—Ask questions about what the person has seen, touched, heard, tasted, or smelled. These details will help your readers vividly imagine the event you are reporting on.

Behavior—What motivated the person to become involved in this project or movement? What do they hope to gain by having their story publicized?

Opinions, values, and feelings—What the person thinks and feels about the topic or event. These questions result in opinionated or personal statements that you, as an objective reporter, most likely will not make in your report. For example, in Model Essay Three, the author quotes from organizer Ellister to express opinions on the subject in a way that would be inappropriate for an objective reporter to do.

Exercise 3B: Report on an Event

Reports show up in many publications—newspapers, magazines, journals, Web logs (blogs) are just some of the places people turn to to read about events and activities under way in their community. Think about the type of event you would like to report on. It could be a trip summary; the happenings of a local or school event, such as a parade, speech, assembly, or rally; a sports game; a party; or another experience in which people are coming together to get something done. Think next about the type of publication in which your report would best appear. Trip summaries, or travelogues, make great fodder for blogs; reports on school events such as sports games or performances are best featured in the school paper.

Before you report on an event, make sure you have done thorough research. Look over all notes from your interviews. Outline a road map for your essay to follow (see exercises in this book on how to outline an essay prior to writing it). Examine where quotations, information, and other details will fit best. After you absorb and organize all the information you have collected, you are ready to write.

News reports tend to be objective, so make sure your writing style is impartial and matter-of-fact. Also, be sure to provide the reader with enough information to visualize the event but not so much that you bombard them with unnecessary or unrelated details. Use the other writing exercises found in this book—on using quotations, writing introductions and conclusions, and gathering research—to help you write the report. Then submit it for publication.

Write Your Own Descriptive Five-Paragraph Essay

Using the information from this book, write your own five-paragraph descriptive essay on an issue related to recycling. You can use the resources in this book for information about topics relating to this subject and how to structure this type of essay.

The following steps are suggestions on how to get started.

Step One: Choose your topic.

The first step is to decide what topic to write your descriptive essay on. Is there any subject that particularly fascinates you about recycling? Is there an issue you strongly support or feel strongly against? Is there a topic you feel personally connected to or one that you would like to learn more about? Ask yourself such questions before selecting your essay topic. Refer to Appendix D: Sample Essay Topics if you need help selecting a topic.

Step Two: Write down questions and answers about the topic.

Before you begin writing, you will need to think carefully about what ideas your essay will contain. This is a process known as *brainstorming*. Brainstorming involves asking yourself questions and coming up with ideas to discuss in your essay. Possible questions that will help you with the brainstorming process include:

- Why is this topic important?
- Why should people be interested in this topic?
- How can I make this essay interesting to the reader?
- What question am I going to address in this paragraph or essay?
- What facts, ideas, or quotes can I use to support the answer to my question?

Questions especially for descriptive essays include:

- Have I chosen a compelling story to examine?
- Have I used vivid details?

- Have I made scenes, events, processes, and issues come alive for my reader?
- What qualities do my characters have? Are they interesting?
- Does my descriptive essay have a clear beginning, middle, and end?
- Does my essay evoke a particular emotion or response from the reader?

Step Three: Gather facts, ideas, and anecdotes related to your topic.

This book contains several places to find information about issues relating to recycling, including the viewpoints and the appendices. In addition, you may want to research the books, articles, and Web sites listed in Section Three or do additional research in your local library. You can also conduct interviews if you know someone who has a compelling story that would fit well in your essay.

Step Four: Develop a workable thesis statement.

Use what you have written down in steps two and three to help you articulate the main point or argument you want to make in your essay. It should be expressed in a clear sentence and make an arguable or supportable point.

Example:

There is no excuse for not imposing mandatory recycling in all American cities.

This could be the thesis statement of a descriptive essay that argues that recycling programs should be mandatory. Supporting paragraphs would explore reasons why the author thinks this and include specific details of the benefits such programs could have on the environment, the economy, and in communities.

Step Five: Write an outline or diagram.
1. Write the thesis statement at the top of the outline.
2. Write roman numerals I, II, and III on the left side of the page; write an A, B, and C under each numeral.

3. Next to each roman numeral, write down the best ideas you came up with in step three. These should all directly relate to and support the thesis statement.

4. Next to each letter write down information that supports that particular idea.

Step Six: Write the three supporting paragraphs.
Use your outline to write the three supporting paragraphs. Write down the main idea of each paragraph in sentence form. Do the same thing for the supporting points of information. Each sentence should support the paragraph of the topic. Be sure you have relevant and interesting details, facts, and quotes. Use transitions when you move from idea to idea to keep the text fluid and smooth. Sometimes, although not always, paragraphs can include a concluding or summary sentence that restates the paragraph's argument.

Step Seven: Write the introduction and conclusion.
See Exercise 2B for information on writing introductions and conclusions.

Step Eight: Read and rewrite.
As you read, check your essay for the following:

✔ Does the essay maintain a consistent tone?
✔ Do all paragraphs reinforce your general thesis?
✔ Do all paragraphs flow from one to the other? Do you need to add transition words or phrases?
✔ Have you quoted from reliable, authoritative, and interesting sources?
✔ Is there a sense of progression throughout the essay?
✔ Does the essay get bogged down in too much detail or irrelevant material?
✔ Does your introduction grab the reader's attention?
✔ Does your conclusion reflect back on any previously discussed material, or give the essay a sense of closure?
✔ Are there any spelling or grammatical errors?

**Section Three:
Supporting
Research
Material**

Facts About Recycling

Editor's Note: These facts can be used in reports to reinforce or add credibility when making important points.

The Environmental Protection Agency says that each year in the United States:

- 5 percent of glass containers are recycled;
- 42 percent of the paper thrown away in the United States is recycled;
- 40 percent of plastic soft drink bottles are recycled;
- 55 percent of aluminum soft drink and beer cans are recycled;
- 57 percent or steel packaging is recycled;
- 52 percent of all major appliances are recycled;
- 88 percent of newspapers are recycled.

According to the Aluminum Company of America (Alcoa):

- 105,784 cans are recycled each minute.
- Recycling keeps 1.7 billion pounds of trash out of landfills.
- Recycling aluminum cans uses 95 percent less energy than making the cans from virgin ore.
- Americans earn approximately $1 billion annually by recycling aluminum cans.
- Recycling a pound of aluminum saves 7.5 kilowatt-hours of electricity.
- Recycling a ton of aluminum saves the equivalent of 14,000 kilowatt-hours of electricity—enough to power an American household for more than fifteen months.

According to the U.S. Department of Energy:

- Recycling and composting divert more than 70 million tons of material from landfills.

- Making a ton of paper from recycled paper saves up to seventeen trees and uses 50 percent less water.

According to the Stanford Recycling Center:
- Each ton of PET plastic containers made from recycled plastic saves 7,200 kilowatt hours.
- One ton of recycled aluminum saves forty barrels of oil.

According to the National Recycling Coalition, the Environmental Protection Agency, and Earth911.org:
- A used aluminum can is recycled and back on the grocery shelf as a new can in as little as sixty days.
- Used aluminum beverage cans are the most recycled item in the United States, but other types of aluminum, such as siding, gutters, car components, storm window frames, and lawn furniture can also be recycled.
- Recycling one aluminum can saves enough energy to run a TV for three hours, which is the equivalent of a half a gallon of gasoline.
- There is no limit to the number of times an aluminum can can be recycled.
- Recycling a single run of the Sunday *New York Times* would save seventy-five thousand trees.
- The average American uses seven trees a year in paper, wood, and other products made from trees. This amounts to about 2 billion trees per year.
- The amount of wood and paper thrown away each year is enough to heat 50 million homes for twenty years.
- Americans use 85 million tons of paper a year; about 680 pounds per person.
- The average household throws away thirteen thousand separate pieces of paper each year. Most is packaging and junk mail.
- Americans use 2.5 million plastic bottles every hour.

- Americans throw away 25 billion Styrofoam coffee cups every year.
- The energy saved from recycling one glass bottle can run a 100-watt light bulb for four hours. It also causes 20 percent less air pollution and 50 percent less water pollution than making a new bottle from raw materials.
- Recycling supports 1.1 million American jobs.

American Opinions About Recycling

A 2008 ABC News/Planet Green/Stanford University poll asked a sample of Americans what they thought was the biggest environmental problem the world faces. Recycling ranked low on the list:

- 25 percent said global warming/climate change;
- 12 percent said air pollution;
- 11 percent said energy problems;
- 7 percent said general pollution;
- 6 percent said toxic substances in the environment;
- 5 percent said water pollution;
- 4 percent said loss of habitat/overdevelopment;
- 4 percent said waste/not enough recycling;
- 14 percent said other;
- 3 percent said none;
- 8 percent said they were unsure.

The poll also found that:

- 67 percent of Americans make an effort to buy products made from recycled materials or that will decompose naturally after being used;
- 32 percent of Americans do not make an effort to buy such products;
- 75 percent of Americans recycle paper, plastic, glass, and/or metal cans in their homes;
- 25 percent do not.

A 2008 Gallup poll asked Americans what changes they had personally made in their shopping and living habits to help protect the environment. Recycling topped the list:

- 39 percent said they started recycling or recycle more;
- 17 percent said they drive less or carpool;
- 14 percent said they buy biodegradable products;
- 10 percent said they use less electricity or conserve energy;
- 9 percent said they drive a more fuel-efficient car;
- 7 percent said they buy and use more "green" products;
- 7 percent said they use more energy-efficient light bulbs;
- 5 percent said they eat more organic or home-grown foods;
- 5 percent said they conserve water;
- 16 percent said they do something else to protect the environment;
- 2 percent said they do nothing;
- 12 percent were unsure if they did anything that helped protect the environment.

Finding and Using Sources of Information

No matter what type of essay you are writing, it is necessary to find information to support your point of view. You can use sources such as books, magazine articles, newspaper articles, and online articles.

Using Books and Articles

You can find books and articles in a library by using the library's computer or cataloging system. If you are not sure how to use these resources, ask a librarian to help you. You can also use a computer to find many magazine articles and other articles written specifically for the Internet.

You are likely to find a lot more information than you can possibly use in your essay, so your first task is to narrow it down to what is likely to be most usable. Look at book and article titles. Look at book chapter titles, and examine the book's index to see if it contains information on the specific topic you want to write about. (For example, if you want to write about recycling electronics and you find a book about garbage and trash in the United States, check the chapter titles and index to be sure it contains information about electronics recycling before you bother to check out the book.)

For a five-paragraph essay, you do not need a great deal of supporting information, so quickly try to narrow down your materials to a few good books and magazine or Internet articles. You do not need dozens. You might even find that one or two good books or articles contain all the information you need.

You probably do not have time to read an entire book, so find the chapters or sections that relate to your topic, and skim these. When you find useful information, copy it onto a note card or notebook. You should look for supporting facts, statistics, quotations, and examples.

Using the Internet

When you select your supporting information, it is important that you evaluate its source. This is especially important with information you find on the Internet. Because nearly anyone can put information on the Internet, there is as much bad information as good information. Before using Internet information—or any information—try to determine whether the source seems to be reliable. Is the author or Internet site sponsored by a legitimate organization? Is it from a government source? Does the author have any special knowledge or training relating to the topic you are looking up? Does the article give any indication of where its information comes from?

Using Your Supporting Information

When you use supporting information from a book, article, interview, or other source, there are three important things to remember:

1. *Make it clear whether you are using a direct quotation or a paraphrase.* If you copy information directly from your source, you are quoting it. You must put quotation marks around the information and tell where the information comes from. If you put the information in your own words, you are paraphrasing it.

Here is an example of a using a quotation:

Many argue that recycling is ineffective because of the large amounts of energy that are expended picking up recycling material and bringing it to recycling centers. As one writer puts it, "Imagine a whole population spending time and money cleaning their garbage and driving it around the neighborhood rather than working or investing in a productive market!" (Bylund).

Here is an example of a brief paraphrase of the same passage:

> Many argue that recycling is ineffective because of the large amounts of energy that are expended picking up recycling material and bringing it to recycling centers. Indeed, when one considers the time, money, and fuel that is expended cleaning, sorting, and collecting items to ready them for recycling, it becomes clear that such efforts would be better spent on a more productive endeavor.

2. *Use the information fairly.* Be careful to use supporting information in the way the author intended it. For example, it is unfair to quote an author as saying, "Recycling uses large amounts of energy" when he or she intended to say, "Recycling uses large amounts of energy, but still represents an overall energy savings." This is called taking information out of context. This is using supporting evidence unfairly.

3. *Give credit where credit is due.* Giving credit is known as citing. You must use citations when you use someone else's information, but not every piece of supporting information needs a citation.
   - If the supporting information is general knowledge—that is, it can be found in many sources—you do not have to cite your source.
   - If you directly quote a source, you must cite it.
   - If you paraphrase information from a specific source, you must cite it.

If you do not use citations where you should, you are *plagiarizing*—or stealing—someone else's work.

Citing Your Sources

There are a number of ways to cite your sources. Your teacher will probably want you to do it in one of three ways:

- Informal: As in the example in number 1 above, tell where you got the information as you present it in the text of your essay.
- Informal list: At the end of your essay, place an unnumbered list of all the sources you used. This tells the reader where, in general, your information came from.
- Formal: Use numbered footnotes or endnotes. Footnotes or endnotes are generally placed at the end of an article or essay, although they may be placed elsewhere depending on your teacher's requirements.

Works Cited

Bylund, Per. "The Recycling Myth." Ludwig von Mises Institute 4 Feb. 2008 < http://mises.org/story/2855 >.

Using MLA Style to Create a Works Cited List

You will probably need to create a list of works cited for your paper. These include materials that you quoted from, relied heavily on, or consulted to write your paper. There are several different ways to structure these references. The following examples are based on Modern Language Association (MLA) style, one of the major citation styles used by writers.

Book Entries

For most book entries you will need the author's name, the book's title, where it was published, what company published it, and the year it was published. This information is usually found on the inside of the book. Variations on book entries include the following:

A book by a single author:
Axworthy, Michael. *A History of Iran: Empire of the Mind*. New York: Basic Books, 2008.

Two or more books by the same author:
Pollan, Michael. *In Defense of Food: An Eater's Manifesto*. New York: Penguin, 2009.
————. *The Omnivore's Dilemma*. New York: Penguin, 2006.

A book by two or more authors:
Ronald, Pamela C., and R.W. Adamchak. *Tomorrow's Table: Organic Farming, Genetics, and the Future of Food*. New York: Oxford University Press, 2008.

A book with an editor
Friedman, Lauri S., ed. *Introducing Issues with Opposing Viewpoints: War*. Detroit: Greenhaven, 2009.

Periodical and Newspaper Entries

Entries for sources found in periodicals and newspapers are cited a bit differently than books. For one, these sources usually have a title and a publication name. They also may have specific dates and page numbers. Unlike book entries, you do not need to list where newspapers or periodicals are published or what company publishes them.

An article from a periodical:
> Hannum, William H., Gerald E. Marsh, and George S. Stanford. "Smarter Use of Nuclear Waste." *Scientific American* Dec. 2005: 84–91.

An unsigned article from a periodical:
> "Chinese Disease? The Rapid Spread of Syphilis in China." *Global Agenda* 14 Jan. 2007.

An article from a newspaper:
> Weiss, Rick. "Can Food from Cloned Animals Be Called Organic?" *Washington Post* 29 Jan. 2008: A06.

Internet Sources

To document a source you found online, try to provide as much information on it as possible, including the author's name, the title of the document, date of publication or of last revision, the URL, and your date of access.

A Web source:
> De Seno, Tommy. *"Roe v. Wade* and the Rights of the Father." The Fox Forum.com 22 Jan. 2009 < http:// foxforum.blogs.foxnews.com/2009/0l/22/deseno_ roe_wade/ > . Accessed May 20, 2009.

Your teacher will tell you exactly how information should be cited in your essay. Generally, the very least information needed is the original author's name and the name of the article or other publication.

Be sure you know exactly what information your teacher requires before you start looking for your supporting information so that you know what information to include with your notes.

Sample Essay Topics

Recycling Is Effective

Recycling Is Ineffective

Recycling Is Environmentally Friendly

Recycling Is Not Environmentally Friendly

Recycling Conserves Resources

Recycling Wastes Resources

Recycling Is Economical

Recycling Is Too Expensive

Recycling Can Help Avert an Energy Crisis

Recycling Will Help Cause an Energy Crisis

Recycling Should Be Mandatory

Recycling Should Not Be Mandatory

The Government Should Lead Efforts to Recycle Electronics

The Government Should Not Lead Efforts to Recycle Electronics

City Governments Should Ban Certain Plastics

City Governments Should Not Ban Certain Plastics

Topics for Descriptive Essays

Portrait of a Landfill

A Look at How Electronics Are Recycled

The Future of Trash

Imagining the World Without Recycling

How to Bring Recycling into Your Life, Home, and Community

The Importance of Recycling

The Myth of Recycling

Organizations to Contact

The editors have compiled the following list of organizations concerned with the issues debated in this book. The descriptions are derived from materials provided by the organizations. All have publications or information available for interested readers. The list was compiled on the date of publication of the present volume; the information provided here may change. Be aware that many organizations take several weeks or longer to respond to inquiries, so allow as much time as possible for the receipt of requested materials.

Container Recycling Institute (CRI)
89 E. Lake Shore Trail, Glastonbury, CT 06033
(202) 263-0999 • Web site: www.container-recycling.org

CRI studies and promotes policies and programs that increase recovery and recycling of beverage containers. CRI plays a vital role in educating policy makers, government officials, and the general public regarding the social and environmental impacts of the production and disposal of no-deposit, no-return beverage containers and the need for producers to take responsibility for their wasteful packaging.

Earth Island Institute (EII)
300 Broadway, Suite 28, San Francisco CA 94133-3312
(415) 788-3666 • fax: (415) 788-7324
Web site: www.earthisland.org

Founded in 1982 by veteran environmentalist David Brower, EII develops and supports projects that counteract threats to the biological and cultural diversity that sustain the environment. Through education and activism, EII promotes the conservation, preservation, and restoration of Earth via activities such as recycling.

Environmental Defense Fund (EDF)

257 Park Ave. South, New York, NY 10010
(212) 505-2100 fax: (212) 505-2375
Web site: www.edf.org

The fund is a nonprofit organization of lawyers, scientists, and economists that works to develop innovative and cost-effective answers to environmental problems. Publications by EDF include "FAQs: Environmental Benefits of Recycled Paper" and "Buy Recycled . . . and Save."

Environment Canada

70 Cremazie St., Gatineau, QC K1A 0H3
(819) 997-2800 • fax: (819) 994-1412
e-mail: enviroinfo@ec.gc.ca • Web site: www.ec.gc.ca

Environment Canada is a department of the Canadian government whose goal is to achieve sustainable development in Canada through environmental protection and conservation. Information about recycling is available on the Web site.

GrassRoots Recycling Network (GRRN)

4200 Park Blvd., #290, Oakland, CA 94602
(510) 531-5523 • Web site: www.grrn.org

GRRN's mission is to eliminate the waste of natural and human resources. The network advocates corporate accountability and public policies that eliminate waste and build sustainable communities. The GRRN Web site includes fact sheets, reports, and articles, including "Composting and Organics: Recycling vs. Bioreactors" and "Beyond Recycling: The Zero Waste Solution."

Greenpeace USA

702 H St. NW, Washington, DC 20001 • (202) 462-1177
e-mail: info@wdc.greenpeace.org
Web site: www.greenpeace.org

Greenpeace is an international environmental organization that aims to protect the oceans and promote a future free of toxic waste. Its publications include *Guide to Greener Electronics* and "Where Does E-Waste Go?"

INFORM
5 Hanover Sq., Floor 19, New York, NY 10004-2638
(212) 361-2400 • Web site: www.informinc.org

INFORM is an organization that looks for innovative practices and technologies to address environmental problems. Reports and fact sheets are available on the Web site, including "The Benefits of Recycling Electronics in the US" and "Greening Garbage Trucks: New Technologies for Cleaner Air."

National Recycling Coalition (NRC)
805 Fifteenth St. NW, Suite 425, Washington, DC 20005
(202) 789-1430 • fax: (202) 789-1431
e-mail: info@nrc-recycle.org
Web site: www.nrc-recycle.org

NRC is a nonprofit organization that aims to advance and improve recycling, reuse, and waste prevention. It seeks to encourage recycling efforts through changes in national policies on energy, waste management, taxes, and transportation. It publishes the e-newsletter *Mobius*.

National Solid Wastes Management Association (NSWMA)
4301 Connecticut Ave. NW, Suite 300, Washington, DC 20008 • (202) 244-4700 • fax: (202) 966-4824
e-mail: membership@envasns.org
Web site: www.nswma.org

NSWMA is a trade association that represents for-profit companies that provide waste collection, recycling, and disposal services. Its goal is to promote environmentally responsible and ethical waste management. Publications on the Web site include *Research Bulletins*, "Profiles in Garbage" fact sheets, and the monthly magazine *Waste Age*.

Natural Resources Defense Council (NRDC)

40 W. Twentieth St., New York, NY 10011
(212) 727-2700 • fax: (212) 727-1773
e-mail: nrdcinfo@nrdc.org • Web site: www.nrdc.org

The council is an environmental group of lawyers and scientists who help write environmental laws and seek to protect the quality of land, air, and water. The NRDC conducts research into topics such as cleaning up the oceans and removing toxic chemicals from the environment. NRDC publishes the quarterly magazine *OnEarth*, a monthly e-mail newsletter, and reports on environmental issues, including *Testing the Waters 2008: A Guide to Water Quality at Vacation Beaches*.

Property and Environment Research Center (PERC)

2048 Analysis Dr, Suite A, Bozeman, MT 59718
(406) 587-9591 • e-mail: perc@perc.org
Web site: www.perc.org

PERC is a research and education foundation that focuses primarily on environmental and natural resource issues. It emphasizes the advantages of free markets and the importance of private property rights regarding environmental protection. Its publications include "Eight Great Myths of Recycling." Other articles about recycling are on the Web site.

Sierra Club

85 Second St., 2nd Floor, San Francisco, CA 94105
(415) 977-5500 • fax: 415-977-5799
e-mail: information@sierraclub.org
Web site: www.sierraclub.org

Founded in 1892, Sierra Club is the oldest grassroots environmental organization in the United States. Its Zero Waste Committee aims to lead the nation in a transition from traditional waste disposal programs to comprehensive recycling systems. The organization publishes *Sierra* magazine six times a year.

UN Environment Programme (UNEP)
900 Seventeenth St. NW, Suite 506, Washington, DC 20006
(202) 785-0465 • Web site: www.unep.org

The goal of the UNEP is to help nations and their citizens improve their quality of life while caring for the environment. Reports on recycling are available on the Web site, and the organization publishes the magazine *Our Planet* three times a year.

U.S. Environmental Protection Agency (EPA)
1200 Pennsylvania Ave. NW, Washington, DC 20460
(202) 272-0167 • Web site: www.epa.gov

The EPA is the government agency charged with protecting human health and safeguarding the natural environment. It works to protect Americans from environmental health risks, enforce federal environmental regulations, and ensure that environmental protection is an integral consideration in U.S. policy. The EPA publishes many reports, fact sheets, and educational materials, including "Electronics: A New Opportunity for Waste Prevention, Reuse, and Recycling" and *Consumer's Handbook for Reducing Solid Waste*.

Bibliography

Books

Gutberlet, Jutta, *Recovering Resources—Recycling Citizenship*. Aldershot, UK: Ashgate, 2008.

Rogers, Heather, *Gone Tomorrow: The Hidden Life of Garbage*. New York: New Press, 2006.

Royte, Elizabeth, *Garbage Land: On the Secret Trail of Trash*. Boston: Back Bay, 2006.

Schlesinger, Mark E., *Aluminum Recycling*. Boca Raton, FL: CRC, 2006.

Scott, Nicky, *Reduce, Reuse, Recycle: An Easy Household Guide*. White River Junction, VT: Chelsea Green, 2007.

Trask, Crissy, *It's Easy Being Green: A Handbook for Earth-Friendly Living*. Layton, UT: Gibbs Smith, 2006.

Zimring, Carl A., *Cash for Your Trash: Scrap Recycling in America*. Piscataway, NJ: Rutgers University Press, 2005.

Periodicals

Aadland, David, and Arthur J. Caplan, "Curbside Recycling: Waste Resource or Waste of Resources?" *Journal of Policy Analysis and Management*, Fall 2006.

Butalia, Urvashi, "Garbage Blues," *New Internationalist*, November 2005.

Carroll, Chris, "High-Tech Trash: Will Your Discarded TV or Computer End Up in a Ditch in Ghana?" *National Geographic*, January 2008.

Clement, Douglas, "Recycling—Righteous or Rubbish?" Federal Reserve Bank of Minneapolis, March 2005. www.heartland.org/custom/semod_policybot/pdf/17273.pdf.

Cockburn, Alexander, "The Dialectics of Revolution . . . uh, Recycling," *Nation*, December 17, 2007.

Deseret News, "Make Recycling a Must," September 29, 2008.

Doughty, Steve, "Now You'll Be Made to Recycle Your Litter in the High Street," *Daily Marl* (UK), May 29, 2008.

Economist, "The Truth About Recycling," June 7, 2007.

Fishman, Charles, "Message in a Bottle," *Fast Company*, December 19, 2007.

Garber, Kent, "Technology's Morning After; Landfills Are Choking on E-Waste, and Christmas Only Makes It Worse," *U.S. News & World Report*, December 31, 2007.

Government Accountability Office, "Recycling: Additional Efforts Could Increase Municipal Recycling," December 2006. www.gao.gov/new.items/d0737.pdf.

Hector, Gordon, "The Waste of Nations," Adam Smith Institute, 2008. www.adamsmith.org/images/pdf/the_waste_of_nations.pdf.

Kalkowski, John, "To Boost Recycling, Make It Profitable," *Converting Magazine*, January 1, 2008.

King, Florence, "Recycling Madness," *National Review*, June 18, 2004.

Kohn, Marek, "Waste: Recycling Rage Hits Our Doorsteps," *New Statesman*, May 29, 2006.

Lambert, Emily, "Waste? Not!" *Forbes*, June 16, 2008.

Langston, Jennifer, "Mandatory Recycling Program Working Well," *Seattle Post-Intelligencer*, March 15, 2006.

McKibben, Bill, "Recycling? Fuhgeddaboudit: Are New Yorkers Right to Think Recycling Is a Waste of Time? *Mother Jones*, May/June 2009.

Naish, John, "The Case for Sufficiency: Our Planet Is Doomed Unless We Learn to Limit Our Consumption," *New Statesman*, March 31, 2008.

Ruggeri, Amanda, "Could the Recession Kill the Recycling Industry? High Costs and Bottled-Up Profits May Push Waste Back to the Landfills," *U.S. News and World Report*, March 13, 2009.

Schoenmann, Joe, "We're Not Recycling Much, and Some Think They Know Why," *Las Vegas Sun*, December 21, 2008.

Teschler, Leland E., "Save Energy: Don't Recycle," *Machine Design*, July 13, 2006.

Weeks, Jennifer, "Future of *Recycling*: Is a Zero-Waste Society Achievable? *CQ Researcher*, December 14, 2007. www.svtc.org/site/DocServer/CQR_Recycling .pdf?docID = 661.

Wente, Margaret, "A Waste of Time and Money," *Reader's Digest*, January 2006.

Wilby, Peter, "Why Capitalism Creates a Throwaway Society: How to Deal with Waste Is the Great Policy Failure of Our Age," *New Statesman*, September 1, 2008.

Web Sites

Earth 911 (www.earth911.org). Earth 911 provides information on recycling in order to help consumers live responsibly and contribute to a sustainable environment. Information on recycling and composting and a monthly newsletter are available on the site.

Global Recycling Network (www.grn.com). This site provides news on recycling and information on environmentally friendly products.

Recycle City (www.epa.gov/recyclecity). This page, maintained by the Environmental Protection Agency, features information about recycling and a kid-friendly game.

RecycleWorks School Recycling Programs (www
.recycleworks.org/schools/schoolpgm.html). Provides
students with information on how to start recycling
programs at their school or college.

Recycling Revolution (www.recycling-revolution.com).
Contains a wealth of information about recycling and
recycling programs.

Reducing Unwanted Mail (www.epa.gov/osw/wycd/
catbook/mail.htm). This page instructs Americans on
how to reduce the number of catalogues, credit card
offers, circulars, and other junk mail they receive.

Reusable Bags.com (www.reusablebags.com). This site
contains information on ways people can reduce their
use of disposable plastic and paper bags.

Index

A

Ackerman, Frank, 38

Alcoa, Inc., 8, 26–30

Aluminum, 8, 26–30, 52

Avellino, Salvatore, 51

B

Batteries, 14

Benjamin, Daniel K., 35, 36, 37

Bio-plastics, 23

Bloomberg, Michael, 35

Blumenfeld, Jared, 44, 46

Bottle bills, 45

Britain, 14

C

Carbon dioxide, 26

Carpooling, 7

Cernansky, Rachel, 18–24

China, 43

D

Dinkins, David, 35

E

Electricity, 27

Energy
  conservation, 8
  consumption, 8–9
  recycling saves, 25–31
  recycling wastes, 32–39

Engineered wood products, 52

Environment
  recycling benefits, 12–17
  recycling can harm, 18–24

Environmental Defense Fund (EDF), 51–52

Europe, 15–16

Extended producer responsibility, 15–16, 45

F

Food scraps, 43, 46

Four Course Compost, 43

Fresh Kills, 36, 37

G

Garbage, 45

Giuliani, Rudy, 35

Glass, 9, 38, 52

Gore, Al, 36

Greenhouse gases, 13, 20, 26, 47

Gunther, Marc, 40–47

H

Hale, Matthew, 13

Hall, Charles Martin, 26

Harrelson, Lowell, 51

Hawken, Paul, 41

I
Inman, Kathleen, 43

L
Lander, Christian, 9
Landfills, 36–37, 47, 50–51
Laws, recycling, 33
Lehr, Jay, 9, 35, 38
Liss, Gary, 45
Logomasini, Angela, 35
Lovins, Amory, 41

M
Mandatory recycling
  is needed, 40–47
  is not needed, 48–53
  in Seattle, 33
Material sorting, *22*, 23
McDonough, William, 41
Methane, 47
Mobro (barge), 41, 51

N
Natural resources, 13–14, 38
Norcal Waste Systems, 42–43, 46

O
Outerbridge, Tom, 24

P
Packaging, 14, 15
Packaging and Packaging
  Waste Directive, 15
Paper, 9, 26, 38, 45, 50

Plastic, 9, 14, 19–24, 38, 45, 52
Poly-Wood, Inc., 52
Product costs, 13
Product design, 46

R
Recycling
  choosing materials for, 14
  city rankings, 44
  costs of, 13, 34–36, 45, 47
  energy consumption and, 8–9
  incentives for, 43–44
  is environmentally friendly, 12–17
  is not environmentally friendly, 18–24
  public views on, 7, 21
  rates of, 29, 33, 34, 41
  saves energy, 25–31
  should be mandatory, 40–47
  should not be manda- tory, 48–53
  significance of, 7–10
  technology, 43
  voluntary, 52
  wastes energy, 32–39
Recycling trucks, 35, 37
Resources, 13–14, 38

S
San Francisco, 41, 42, 43–44
Sandbrook, Richard, 38

Sangiacomo, Mike, 42
Scrap usage, 27
Seattle, 33–34, 38
Seventh Generation, 23
Shaw, Michael D., 48–53
Sheehan, Bill, 15
Sorting, *22*, 23
Steel, 14, 26

T
Taylor, Jerry, 36, 38
Technology, 43
Teschler, Leland E., 8
Thayer, James, 32–39
Tierney, John, 50, 51
Toyota, 41

V
Voluntary recycling, 52

W
Wal-Mart, 41
Waste & Resources
  Action Programme, 13
Waste disposal, 41–43
Wastepaper, 43
Whitaker, Greg, 8
Wittbecker, Greg, 25–31

Z
Zeller, Tom, Jr., 9,
  12–17
Zero waste, 41, 45

Picture Credits

About the Editor

Lauri S. Friedman earned her bachelor's degree in religion and political science from Vassar College in Poughkeepsie, New York. Her studies there focused on political Islam. Friedman has worked as a nonfiction writer, a newspaper journalist, and an editor for more than ten years. She has extensive experience in both academic and professional settings.

Friedman is the founder of LSF Editorial, a writing and editing business in San Diego. She has edited and authored numerous publications for Greenhaven Press on controversial social issues such as Islam, genetically modified food, women's rights, school shootings, gay marriage, and Iraq. Every book in the *Writing the Critical Essay* series has been under her direction or editorship, and she has personally written more than twenty titles in the series. She was instrumental in the creation of the series, and played a critical role in its conception and development.